HIGH LIFE — LOW LIFE

HIGH LIFE
LOW LIFE

Taki / Jeffrey Bernard

Introduction by Richard West

Edited by Cosmo Landesman

Jay Landesman Limited — London

FOR ALEXANDER CHANCELLOR

First published in Great Britain in 1981 by
JAY LANDESMAN LIMITED, 159 Wardour Street, London W1.

ISBN 0 905150 27 9

Photo-composition by Nicholas Lumsden.
Printed and bound in Great Britain.

CONTENTS

EDITOR'S ACKNOWLEDGEMENTS

A special debt of thanks is due to Alexander Chancellor, the editor of *The Spectator* wherein most of the articles in this book first appeared, and without him the book would not have been possible. Thanks also to the *New Statesman*, *Private Eye*, *Esquire*, *Punch*, and the *American Spectator* for permission to reproduce pieces.

Cosmo Landesman

INTRODUCTION: *Richard West*

We fans of Taki and Jeffrey Bernard have often debated how to define the frontier dividing High Life and Low Life. After all, both our authors have much the same hobbies and weaknesses. Take gambling, for instance. While Jeff is a chronic backer of horses — and wrote on the subject under the name of 'Colonel Mad' — Taki prefers the tables and used to live in Mayfair because, as he here confesses — 'I could roll out of bed and be at Aspinall's and gambling in exactly three minutes if I was really pushed . . . A daily fix of chemmy was something I could not go without'. Both Taki and Jeff are devoted to sport, on the one hand polo, tennis, American football and ski-ing; on the other hand snooker, soccer and boxing. Indeed Jeff was for a short period a professional fighter; Taki represents Greece at karate. Both men still occasionally get into fights with different results, dependent on age and condition . . . Taki recently came off best from an affray with a diplomat in a Paris night-club, while Jeff got the worse of things after asking a Scottish football supporter to please play his bag-pipes a fraction less *forte*.

Nor is difference of High Life and Low Life simply a question of money, since Jeff mixed frequently with the rich; and Taki has friends who are chronically fleeing the bailiffs and bookmakers. After all, Taki and Jeff know one another.

But difference of income conditions the travelling habits of Taki and Jeff; and it is here, in geography that we see the difference of style between High Life and Low Life. Although Taki is Greek, he is critical of his countrymen, and indeed was sentenced to prison once *in absentia* in some political row; so he visits there seldom, and usually in the safety of a yacht. The dangers of dry land are found in the account given here of an effort to murder him by persons unknown. Most of his time seems to be spent in New York, London, Gstaad, the ski-ing resorts, with just occasional ventures into the lands, like Yugoslavia, which the ancient Greeks defined as barbaric.

Our Low Life reporter Jeffrey Bernard takes the view that the cost of an international air ticket could much better be spent on essentials like vodka and horses. He does here record a trip to Barbados, where he met Sir Gordon Richards, and Manchester where he studied and brooded upon the stupendous pub whose ceiling is decorated with 500 pairs of knickers. (It is a moving chapter.) Otherwise Jeff's experience is roughly divided between the racing village of Lambourn and Soho, where he is normally to be found at the Shaftesbury Avenue end of the York Minster (or French House as it now absurdly calls itself) and the Cambridge Circus end of the Coach and Horses (prop Norman Balon).

Their natural habitat makes for the difference in life style of Taki and Jeff. Each blends quite naturally into his surroundings. The last time I met Taki, at lunch in the Savoy, he began by explaining that he had left a party only at ten o'clock that morning; he then recognised and saluted Princess Margaret at the next but one table; then he greeted a famous financier who explained that he, the financier, had just chartered one of the Taki family's 100,000 ton tankers. I was impressed, not to say awed.

When I last met Jeffrey Bernard in Soho, he had just been having a drink with two of his ex-wives; he was listening to a stall-holder's complaints that people in Brixton prison cheated at cards; and he was saying that during this gap in the racing season, they ought to revive a meeting in south London where half-starved cats were matched in a steeplechase through a ground floor and garden to get at the food at the winning post.

Much of Low Life revolves around pubs and how to behave in them: Jeff is a stickler for etiquette, such as: 'If Guvnor allows you to stay after closing time you don't waste his time by drinking halves of bitter and you include him in every round.' Much of High Life revolves round clubs where stimulants are imbibed not through the mouth but the nose. 'Life is better with coke says the familiar motto and millions of drippy-nosed owners tend to agree.' 'Given the widespread use of cocaine among the beautiful people,' Taki explains, 'there is hardly a chic party given nowadays that doesn't sound like a hay fever clinic during the month of June.'

In his chronicles of the High Life, Taki cannot conceal a sense that things are not what they were; that the wrong people are taking over. 'When Aspinall sold his club to the Playboy Club and left for the country, things changed. Lucan got so upset that he made one of the greatest gaffes of mistaken identity I know. Dominic Elwes couldn't take any longer and simply killed himself, and Charles Benson went further than any of us; he got married and began hanging around with royals.' And now the purlieus of High Life have fallen prey to South American polo players, North American homosexuals, above all to those with the dope. Now a Bianca, a Mick, or even a Jackie are not worth three grams of pure Peruvian snow.'

Both Taki and Jeff are at their best on the normally difficult subject of sex. Taki mourns for the once lovely island of Mykonos where now the 'white-voiled, baggy-trousered and shirted, patchouli-scented young men cruise the main square looking for caftan-dressed German tycoons shopping for the latest gold chain or bracelet.' He mourns the demise of Madame Claude's brothel in Paris, closed by the communists; and of the London high-class tart, spoiled by the Arabs. Jeffrey Bernard tips his hat to the 5'6", one-legged man who in Cornwall some years ago was accused of raping a 17 stone 16 year-old virgin in the front seat of a car parked outside an abattoir. One of Jeff's essays in this book contains the memorable observation: 'Insanity is like VD. You catch it by going to bed with people.' Whereas Jeff tends to start with particular instances before coming to his conclusions — such as the one just quoted — Taki will often begin with an aphorism. 'Happiness, said Saint-Just a century ago, is a new concept in Europe,' from which he goes on to advise us: 'Don't be a groupie and open your house to Jack, Warren, Ryan, Marisa and the rest of the Hollywood-Halston set. Don't drop your aitches on purpose . . .' Good advice, I am sure, for Taki and Jeffrey Bernard have between them written a standard book on the etiquette of the High and Low Life.

Having read all these essays as they appeared in the *Spectator*, I found then even more delightful brought together in this book. I read it and laughed out loud on a Sunday evening in Belfast.

HIGH LIFE — LOW LIFE

1. THE GOTHS AT THE GATE: THE HIGH LIFE UNDER SIEGE: *Taki*

TRENDS

Happiness, said Saint-Just a century ago, is a new concept in Europe. Modern anthropologists define it in different ways. Like keeping up, or being trendy. Take the typical young girl today. A pair of tight jeans with pencil-thin legs, a hot-green tube top, a purple belt, a yellow plastic bracelet, high-heeled shoes, frizzy hair and two bright spots of pink rouge on her cheeks. She could be the daughter of a duke or a postman. One could never tell them apart. Even the dropping of an H or two is not a sure sign of one's patrimony. After all, the trendiest thing today is to speak like a worker. Look over your shoulder and you'll see thousands of happy nobs and proles streaking happily astride their common trendiness towards the Eighties' Nirvana. To be in is to be happy. And as Spinoza said, happiness is not a reward but a state of mind.

The pop culture of today makes it *de rigueur* to keep up. It used to be intensely American to hanker after the new and different. No longer. Ever since the Swinging Sixties, London has replaced New York as the centre of collective individualism, like punk culture and rebellion. It is an urban phenomenon, spread about by the television to hundreds of thousands of breathlessly waiting prospective consumers, compulsively eager to sink half their pay check or allowance in some trifle that in months or weeks will be as dead as yesterday's campaign promise. The fads, needless to say, are churned out by a Trojan horse called the economy. All those nice people from Marks and Sparks, Harrods, Conrans and Halston. And Adidas. There are Adidas to jog with, Adidas to play basket ball with, Adidas to exercise with, Adidas to relax with, Adidas to walk with. Not being aware of this I bought a pair of them and played tennis with them. After one set I had pulled a muscle. 'Dummy,' said my doctor, 'you played tennis with jogging Adidas, they're only good to run forward with.'

See what I mean about happiness. I looked like a fool and, worse, I felt like one. Now I have four pairs and spend half my time trying to figure out what I will do during the day in order not to pull a muscle with the wrong shoe. Cynics call my predicament fad-following.

Whereas the trend setters used to be society figures and politicians, such are the depths to which both groups have degenerated that Hollywood types are now the leaders of the conspicuous consumers, or clothesaholics. Diane Keaton, a homely girl who in normal times would never get the boy, popularised the 'Annie Hall Look'. She donned men's waist-coats and ties, although real trendies had been doing it for years. Which brings us to Woody Allen. He has made losers winners by expertly manipulating us to like the man who never gets the girl. So now you have a situation in which to be strong is out, to be good almost criminal, and to be a patriot worse than child molesting. No wonder a lot of old type movie stars like George Sanders preferred to commit suicide.

For a trend to catch on you need only one condition. Publicity. And we all know how easy it is to get that today. There are more PR people around than there are Arabs, and they tend to give more parties than Marie Antoinette ever did. Big Brother dictates that in order to keep up one has to wear Halston, go to discos, admit that God is dead, be gay, ridicule the military, genuflect for oil-riches and jog.

So don't fall for the 1984 fashion trap. Don't be a working woman. Don't be a new man, meaning a man who is ready to forget male dominance and pick up a dish cloth. Don't insist on eating everywhere Italian. Don't protest about the same things the high priestess of contrived causes and publicity, Jane Fonda, protests about. Don't wear bright colours and broad shoulders. Don't be a groupie and open your house to

Jack, Warren, Ryan, Marisa and the rest of the Hollywood-Halston set. Don't drop your H's on purpose. Don't buy high tech. Don't take up transcendental meditation and other such phoney pursuits. Sign up with a good karate teacher instead. It is a great exercise for both sexes and can come in handy too. Finally, never buy or do anything that newspapers or magazines advise you to do.

EVER UPWARD

Social mountaineers, once treated with contempt by their peers, are now becoming a dominant force in international society. And riding on the coat-tails of upwardly mobile folk, in their frenzied dash toward social Nirvana, are the groupies that 'sixties pop culture phenomenon, the curse of the 'nouveau riche' and the famous. In fact, the two are now symbiotic. 'All groupies are social climbers and vice versa,' was the way Lord Charles Churchill explained it.

'Not necessarily so,' responds John Aspinall, wild animal breeder, game park owner and proprietor of Aspinall's, London's most exclusive gaming club. 'Some groupies prefer to remain followers all their lives as they are social primates; the real leaders show their strength early and drag the tribe upward with them.'

Whatever the scientific argument's result may be, there are now more social climbers surrounded by groupies than ever before, and there are no more parties in which the climbers don't dominate. Even the most exclusive of gatherings have been all but taken over by the Himalayan set. 'The more exclusive the gathering the better I like it,' says Louis Basualdo, a six goal handicap Argentinian polo player. 'Cono, here in England it is so easy, the women are always after us, and the husbands smile. All you need is a mallet and a gomina hair.'

And although Basualdo might be accused of arrogance, it is a fact that South American polo players have been causing havoc while cutting a wide swathe among the female popu-lation in English country houses. Social observers, in the meantime, have not missed the irony. It was only twenty years ago that the late, unlamented Aly Khan was quoted as saying: 'They called me a nigger and a wog and I boffed their wives.'

However unpleasant, such attitudes proved that despite the loss of Empire, England still possessed some pride. Because Aly Khan, although connected with horses, was not only called names he was also refused access to certain houses. Today all this is past. As one Volvo estate owner put it: 'we deserve everything we are getting; not only do they take our wives but, more important, drink our port and smoke our cigars.'

Given the fact that the first social climber in history used her physical attributes for advancement, the Argentinians are hardly original in their climb. The real social phenomenon is the pop culture groupie-climber.

Mark and Lola Winters entertain in their opium den in South Kensington. Lola scans Heathrow's discarded files and checks the best hotels to find which celebrities are staying there. Mark spends his days in his art gallery telephoning people who are about to give a party, and asking them to come to dinner on the same day.

When the victim refuses but invites them instead to join him, Mark asks if he can bring, say, Bianca Jagger or Jack Nicholson, 'who just happen to be in town and we cannot leave them alone.' Once safely at the party the couple protect their precious cargo like Swiss guards. The only people allowed access are photographers and social peers. Then the cargo is dangled as bait.

When dope became *de rigueur* for the beautiful people during the 'sixties, social mountaineers were quick to grasp its importance. Now, a Bianca, a Mick, or even a Jackie are not worth three grams of pure Peruvian snow. Acapulco gold and Peruvian pure have in fact managed to save enormous amounts of money for the climbers. Why go into the needless expense of renting chateaux, yachts, flying over orchestras, or giving balls in horrible places like Venice when all one needs is a pad to crash out, loud music, a few straws and a pipe. If you cannot get to the summit of your social ambition, you are sure to get the son or daughter.

SNORTERS

Life is better with coke says the familiar motto and millions
of drippy-nosed owners tend to agree. Starting with Hollywood, where being without it is commensurate to social
leprosy, all the way across America and western Europe, the
use of cocaine has reached epidemic-like proportions. And it
is indicative of the moral degeneracy of these egalitarian
times that the mood-altering drug once used by the nobility to
enhance conversation and sexual activity, has now become the
moving force among dim-witted jet setters, monosyllabic
rock musicians, social climbing rag traders and Washington
bureaucrats. And, of course, everyone connected with the
world of entertainment and fashion. The high that cocaine
gives lasts about twenty minutes. It is a euphoric type of upper
but conditional to the mood of the person taking it. In other
words, it accentuates one's feelings. As experienced snorters
insist, one never sniffs when down. Historically, coke goes
back a long way. In 2525 BC Chinese doctors prescribed it as
medicine. Talleyrand allegedly used it throughout his life, and
was reported to grumble that the 'Corsican's moods could use
some of the happy dust.' Even Queen Victoria is said to have
used it to relieve the pain of menstrual cramps.

Whatever its medical benefits may be, it is nevertheless
a proven fact that long time use results in loss of memory,
extreme paranoia, and extensive damage to the nasal
membranes. In fact, trendy plastic surgeons now find restor-
ing 'burned out' noses more profitable than lifting larger parts
of the human anatomy. Unlike amphetamines, which it greatly
resembles, cocaine is subtle and intellectual. There is no
clouding of the senses, hallucination or spaced-out feeling.
Just a smooth coating of confidence and energy. This is the
main reason, along with trendiness, that so many businessmen are taking it. Coke, needless to say, is a capitalist drug.
As there is ritual involved, the richer the taker, the more
expensive the props. Thin lines of white powder are cut and
spread out with a gold razor and then snorted through a gold
spoon. Junkies simply pour it on the cleavage between their
thumb and index finger and sniff it uncut. One can tell easily

how rich or well brought up the snorter is just by looking at him sniffing. In its pure form coke would probably be harmless. It gives a pleasant buzz and puts one to sleep. The trouble is, finding the Holy Grail is easier than finding pure coke. The pushers are greedy and cut the stuff with every piece of filth imaginable. And that, in turn, gets all those noses running.

Given the widespread use of cocaine among the beautiful people, there is hardly a chic party given nowadays that doesn't sound like a hay fever clinic during the month of June. Lavatories of 'with it' night clubs are worse. One has to enter with a surgical mask as if in an asbestos plant during an explosion. Masses of humanity sniff, snort, sneeze, cough and expectorate. One popular London club has even taken out the toilet bowls as redundant. Sociologists believe that cocaine has not only become the supreme status-symbol,it also has changed the very fibre of aesthetic love. Where once intellect, charm, and physical beauty were the major attractions they are now worthless if not accompanied by at least an ounce of the happy dust. Ironically, coke affects the sexes differently. Men get turned on physically, women mentally. In England, the widespread use of coke has turned things topsy-turvy. Now men want to go to bed and women simply want to chat.

Although it is difficult to gauge accurately the prevalence of cocaine use among the rich and famous, it is safe to say that the majority of the entertainment world takes it. Art dealers buy it but only to offer it to clients. The one institution that does not indulge is the Fourth Estate.

PARADISE LOST

Vouliagmeni

This is the plushest resort in Greece. Ten miles east of Athens, it is a complex of bungalows, hotels, restaurants, swimming pools and marinas, all built on a promontory surrounded by beach. I first came here during the war. In those days it took about three hours by car. Sometimes more, sometimes less. Everything depended on the mood of the Germans, Italians or of the Morris car my father had. There were unpaved roads, with road blocks manned by the Germans and Italians. Sometimes they would ask a lot of questions, sometimes they would simply wave us by. The Morris behaved similarly. Sometimes it ran, sometimes it didn't. But even after all the hardships that the Germans, Italians and British engineering could throw at us, once at Vouliagmeni I never heard anyone complain. The place was simply paradise.

In those pre-polluted days one hardly noticed things that now impress us, such as the whiteness of the beach or the clearness of the water. I don't think in all my travels I have ever seen a place even approach the colour of the sea and sand of Vouliagmeni. Even after the occupation very few people ventured there. Five miles closer to the city there was a chic beach the then beautiful people favoured. Vouliagmeni had a taverna called Olymbitis, which served fresh fish and chips, and ice-cold white retsina. In those days it was chic to drink wine and, whenever possible, whisky. Retsina was for the masses, and the Olymbitis crowd were in a way the first punk Greeks. Needless to say all the people who went there were rich because public transport did not venture further than the chic beach. Already in 1946 there were Fords and Buicks leaving their tyre tracks and petrol leaks on Vouliagmeni's beaches.

The years went by, the Civil war was won by the Nationalists and reconstruction began. In 1956, during the international tennis tournament, which was a yearly fixture in Athens then, I took two Italian friends of mine to my favourite beach. Giorgio Fachini and Umberto Bergamo were both ranked in their country's top ten throughout the Fifties. When they swam at Vouliagmeni that day, however, they forgot all about tennis, rankings and responsibilities.

In 1961, the then prime minister, Constantine Caramanlis, decided Greece needed tourism. The place he hit on first was Vouliagmeni. Olymbitis was torn down by bulldozers and fresh fish was replaced by canapés. The Astir Hotel Company, a subsidiary of the National Bank of Greece, erected bungalows, deluxe hotels and the rest of the trappings needed to survive among the rich.

In 1962, America's First Lady, Jackie Kennedy came to Greece on a holiday, and for a little shopping on the side. Caramanlis was so impressed by her that he decided to give her a choice of real estate, a promontory running parallel to Vouliagmeni. But he didn't figure on the unholy alliance of capital and commune. For once both the Right and Left shouted in unison in parliament. Caramanlis had to withdraw his offer.

This year, trying to recapture images of my youth I have returned to Vouliagmeni. It turns out to be almost the same, but not quite. For one, my neighbours are Arabs who keep spitting in front of my cabana as if it were a spitoon. Their children do biggies in the swimming pool and the place has to be drained after every meal. Trying to swim in the sea is a dodgy business. If the jelly fish don't get you the speeding motor boats will. The Greeks staying in the complex look like grocers, act like butchers, and tend to make some of our Arab brethren look almost noble. The staff, however, has remained the best in Greece, undermanned, underpaid, but always kind and helpful. My suggestion is that the Bank kicks out the Arabs and nouveaux, installs the staff as guests, drains the bay and fills it up with Evian water.

TROJAN HORSES

English gentlemen's clubs, already in their death throes, are suffering the ultimate indignity. In order to ensure their survival they are electing as members foreigners in general and Americans in particular. Needless to say, this heresy has not stopped the rot. On the contrary, the cure is killing the patient faster than the disease. What club authorities did not take into account when the practice first began was the extreme snobbery afflicting all foreigners, especially when in England.

This foreign poise, in the meantime, has managed to debauch the infinite subtlety which makes an English gentleman and replace it with its American counterpart: an unpraised nose, a locked jaw and an overpowering smell of deodorant.

Although the decline of gentlemen's clubs is recent, the first signs can be traced to the period after the war. That is when well-meaning but misguided members — most of whom were suffering from shell-shock — bandied things like 'comrades in arms' around. Some comrades were admitted and that is when the trouble really started.

When Labour's tax structure made sure the only asset English gentlemen were allowed to keep was their dignity, clubs opened their doors to more and more foreigners. And, appropriately, the foreign devils reverted to type. Now the place resembles Park Avenue, or Piraeus, with grotesque American women screaming for their husbands to come out and help with the shopping bags, or fat Greek businessmen lamenting tanker rates while loudly sipping Turkish coffee with upraised diamond pinkies. To make things worse, the so-called American disease has spread, like a cancer, to the English countryside. More and more wives are demanding their husbands come home after work or else. In fact, the else has happened. Some clubs have not only opened their doors to the fairer sex, they even allow it to spend the night.

Given the above facts, some pessimists believe that clubs might even be sued for discrimination by feminists. And they point out that appeasement usually leads to worse excesses. The main trouble, however, remains the constant striving for upward mobility by the foreigners. As everyone knows social climbers are ruthless and never relaxed. Their sensory devices are on constant alert thus not conducive to club atmosphere. And the English don't help. Throwing around the kind of adjectives they used to, they insult the newly discovered dignity of the foreign element, which now gives as good as it gets by calling the English 'tap outs' and beggars.

As the first ingredient of an English gentleman is lack of responsibility, the foreigners' observance of superficial rules and puritanical viewpoints adds to the already tense climate. As the secretary of a St James's club said to me: 'Our foreign members try to emulate our local ones by being stiff and formal. They become very boring instead.' The classic case of being more English than the English and boring everyone in sight is that of a Greek brother act.

Having had the misfortune of a very common father — even by Greek standards — the brothers decided to become gentlemen once rich. Leaving America which was already full of social climbers — thus very competitive — they settled in England. After studying the mannerisms of what they thought were gents they applied to a club. To their surprise they were elected as no one knew them. But soon they were dubbed Arsenic and Old Lace and shunned by everyone, including Arsenic's English wife. The reason? Very simple. The brothers acted like Hollywood's version of a gentleman. One was rude, the other silent. In fact, throughout their stay in England not a sound came from the silent one except for the occasional cough. But there was a happy ending. They used their club as a stepping stone and finally got into an American one.

Which brings us to another indignity. Foreigners are using their English clubs as Trojan Horses. As they are accepted here automatically, they use the reciprocal agreements between English and foreign clubs to crash places in which they are unwanted. One very old Danish queen has infiltrated Paris's Jockey Club in this manner. It is the Americans, though, who abuse the club system the most by giving it such importance. As an example I will mention a personal experience. A friend of mine called Michael Thomas recently joined White's. Thomas is a very amusing if somewhat vulgar American. Upon election he rang my brother in New York and asked him if he would pick up a White's club tie when next in London. My brother, who is not a member, replied that he would do so with pleasure but that he didn't know White's had club ties. 'Yes, I know,' answered Thomas and hung up.

2. 'FINGS AIN'T WHAT THEY USED TO BE': THE DECLINE OF THE LOW LIFE: *Jeffrey Bernard*

TREASURE ISLAND

By and large I've met a better class of person in the gutter than I have in the drawing room. This isn't inverted snobbery on my part it's just that I've always found people who skate on thin ice to be that much sharper, keener and sympathetic than those who've got life sewn up and who can look their bank manager in the eye. There's nothing like the experience of being broke to keep a man on his toes and if he can stay on them and still cultivate a highly defined sense of the absurd then he's the man for me. Those people who give me the impression that they've just stepped out of *Vogue* or *House and Garden* seem to me to be utterly out of touch with reality and, cushioned against life, pretty bloody ignorant of it. Of course, *Vogue* may well be reality to them but it's a reality that, from what I've seen of it, has precious little to do with all those people out there beyond the gravel drive. But it's pillars of respectability that I must thank for kindling my interest in the low life in the beginning.

At around about the age of thirteen I discovered Soho and it's been a downhill struggle ever since. If you're wondering how such a dump could possibly have gripped me and seduced me as it did then you didn't know it as it was in those days. To step out of both the classroom and my mother's Dresden littered drawing room into that was to step on to Disneyland, Pleasure Island, Treasure Island — you name it. What an incredible mixture I'd stumbled across. Poets, painters, prostitutes, bookmakers' runners, Bohemians, bums, café

philosophers, crooks and cranks. George Barker, Dylan
Thomas, Sidney Graham, Francis Bacon, Lucien Freud, the
'Roberts' Colquhoun and McBryde, 'French' Vera, Sid the
Swimmer, Ironfoot Jack, Nina Hamnett, Sylvia Gough,
Mandrake Boris Watson, Muriel Belcher, Gaston Berlemont,
Frank Norman, Italian Albert Dimes, Jack Spot, John Minton
and a hundred more.

Of course, it was too good to miss a moment of it so getting
a job was out of the question and in any case what on earth had
two years at the naval college equipped me to do? I did the odd
job obligatory in the life of a bum — navvying, dish washing,
even a spell in a coal mine and then in a boxing booth in a
fairground, but I was always drawn back to Soho who was
always there waiting with open arms and legs.

Once upon a time, when Atticus was Henry Fielding, when
there was a restaurant upstairs at the French pub, when veal
escalope, chips and spaghetti was 3/6d in Fava's, when you
could have a night out in Soho and end up drunk, penniless
and alone on only £1, then Soho had real quality.

But now Soho is dead. Massive injections of advertising
executives with pocket bleepers and a taste for cheap wine
and large doses of television, film commercial producers
dressed in denim suits and with a liking for Chicken *sopresa*
at £1.95 a portion served by Sycophantic hordes of semi-
nautical looking waiters all thinking they are Rossanno Brazzi,
have finally killed off what was just about the best part of
London for anyone who never saw virtue in work for its own
sake.

Many of the great Soho characters are all dead and who
can blame them? Their replacements are monstrous. The
Shaftesbury Avenue end of the York Minster has become like
a peep show at a fairground. There's no bearded lady but
there's a midget salesman who makes his pocket money by
gambling with people when they're drunk. There's a man who
was thrown out of the police force because of brutality. Yes,
you heard me, brutality. There's a publisher who gives 30p
advances and a writer who takes them, and I could go on.

Of course, I know it's the height of the season and a lot of
the better people are away, including the woman who once

tried to rape Errol Flynn on the corner of Old Compton Street
and the Charing Cross Road — luckily for him he'd already
had a hard day at the studios — and Brian the Burglar won't
be back till February. Nevertheless, there hasn't been a
controversial fight or abortion since the days of the Caves de
France when some of us made a book on Phil Drake's Derby
and then couldn't pay out until 'No Nickers Joyce' came to
our rescue.

The first signs of Soho's decline were visible twenty years
ago. Bearded Les got a job and if that wasn't enough of a
sign I got married to what they used to call a 'nice' girl. Then
there was the strange case of Chicago Dave repaying a loan
He said it was insurance. The King of the pornographers
opened an antique shop. 'Dirty Dave' started washing and
they switched from chess to five-card stud in the Mandrake
Club.

Now poets are actually having to write poetry. Strip clubs,
dirty bookshops and amusement arcades spring up like weeks
and a lot of people blame the town planners for the decline of
Soho but the truth is it's the people that have gone to seed.

HOST-ILE

Last week, in the Coach and Horses in Greek Street, I asked to
see the menu so as to find out what was cooking for lunch.
Norman Balon, the landlord, threw it at me. Later, when I
asked to pay by cheque, he refused me because I hadn't got
my banker's card on me. This, in spite of the fact that he's
previously cashed many cheques for me over the years. Two
trivial incidents really, both the consequence of a mediocre
education but intended as wit by this misguided man. The
point is, the English pub — and God knows I've lovingly
kept my finger on its pulse for some time now — isn't just in
decline, it's reached rock bottom.

During the same week I was actually driven out of a pub in
Fleet Street with acute earache by a landlord who insisted on
detailing the day's weather to me and, in Lambourn two days
later, I was driven out of one pub by a too loud jukebox,

another since they wanted to charge me 22 pence for a split of soda and yet another because the barmaid would keep button-holing me so as to enquire what might win the Cheltenham Tote Gold Cup. If one's pocket isn't being assaulted one's ears are. Come to think of it, the eyes suffer a little too when they're confronted with carpets designed by council house mentalities, formica, plastic dolls from Majorca and notices which say that you don't have to be mad to work there but that it helps. More to the point, you don't have to be mad to drink there but it helps.

The root of the trouble lies in the fact that publicans have got far too big for their hush puppies. They no longer know their place, which is behind the bar providing a service. They all want to be 'characters' nowadays and even the nicest ones seem convinced that they're a Jack the Lad to a man. One of the more hypocritical traits displayed by these people is their objection to bad language. By bad language they mean swear-ing. And yet look at their language. The words and phrases are quite disgusting. 'Squire — neck of the woods — ding dong (for Bells whisky) — my better half — tincture — at this moment in time — gee and tee — long time no see — I've only got one pair of hands — similar? — don't tell my bank manager — cold enough for you?' etc.

I used to think that pubs were for the relief of pain but it seems, with very few exceptions, that only the Irish still realise this. They actually apprentice boys to become barmen because they know just how important a business it is to serve drinks speedily and correctly without referring to strikes, abortion laws, the Arsenal, Mrs Thatcher, the winter of 1947, or yesterday's near win at the betting shop.

The situation in Berkshire has now become so desperate that, next week, I am taking one of London's most civilised publicans on a guided tour of the Lambourn area in the hope that he will buy a free house down there. There's one that's just been sold for something in the region of £125,000. There's another on offer for the same amount and one near Newbury that the guvnor's asking no less than £160,000 for. One must therefore assume that such people are salting away something like £500 per week if such places are successful. No wonder

that the attitude is a take it or leave it one. No wonder the
bread is plastic and the sausages limp and the bitter off.

We do have one man in the sticks, though, who is monstrous
to a degree where he's probably quite right about the other
side of the coin. Customers can be as ghastly as publicans
and this man is sure of it. He regards his pub as a club. Any
passing trade he doesn't like the look of, i.e. anyone who
doesn't look as though he drinks to excess, he doesn't serve.
He gives them a dirty look and tells them, 'Not in here thank
you, sir. You'll find a nice little pub that'll suit you just down
the road.'

I suppose they're usually so awful because being a publican
must be such a heady business. Stars in their tiny firmaments
surrounded, by and large, by customers who'll put up with
almost anything. And the worst thing about the price of drink
today is that it's given these people an inflated idea of their
own importance. I imagine it's simply a matter of time before
the customer — as a species — will develop and grow a fore-
lock to be tugged at by publicans.

AROUND TOWN

Circumstance plus an inaccurate watch had me waiting for
someone for a solid half-hour last Monday at the entrance of
Earls Court tube station. If you don't think that London and
its inhabitants and visitors are going down the drain try loiter-
ing in the Earls Court Road yourself. The procession of
shoppers, travellers and people out strolling was a squalid
pageant. Inside the station entrance there was a young man
pimping for a local hotel, a wino with a face like a burst strawberry and sipping wine out of a bottle, and a young couple
selling copies of *News Line* and looking so intensely dedicated
to their cause that it made you yawn to glance at them. The
road itself now seems to be lined with those self-service
grocery stores that keep open at odd hours and which stitch
you up for the privilege and the pavements are blocked by
bewildered looking foreign students weighed down by ruck-
sacks and seemingly wondering whether they hadn't all made

the most ghastly mistake in coming to Earls Court at all. Mind you, Earls Court to a foreigner probably sounds fairly posh and it may well be that they think it's going to be a sort of English Versailles, but a glance into one of the restaurants where you can buy salmonella to take away must surely put them right in double quick time.

I'm wondering where the hell they all go to when they become disillusioned with Earls Court. Carnaby Street perhaps. Now that is a wow. They've got people in Carnaby Street who actually get rich selling rubbish, cheese-cloth shirts, coffee-table games or whatever. I just can't believe that there's anything wrong with the economy of this country when people can afford to buy silver balls suspended on string and then spend their evenings banging them together to the accompaniment of a group of recording psychopaths. Everyone to their own thing.

After Carnaby Street I imagine our tourist, his rucksack by now bursting with quality. English gifts and his stomach-lining soothed by the balm of a Wimpy and cup of instant coffee, trudges on to the glamour and excitement of jolly old boozy Bohemian Soho. You can imagine their disappointment when they discover that Dylan Thomas isn't able to make an appearance in the York Minster today. Never mind, there's lots more to see before going back to Earls Court or Padding-ton to find a bed for the night. For one thing everyone just has to take in a few typical English pubs like Ward's Irish House in Piccadilly and then go and poison the ducks in St James's Park with Charles Forte leftovers, to say nothing of taking a snap of our famous afternoon drinking club the House of Commons. Anyone who spends their holidays trudging around Europe should still have enough stamina after all that to inspect Chelsea and the Kings Road. To think that everyone you bump into is simply oozing artistic talent is a sobering thought unless, of course, you've had a drop too much of our wonderful pressurised beers. A slow wander past more trendy jeans and cheese-cloth shirt shops will bring our sweating, numbed, rucksack bearer dangerously close to Earls Court but thankfully to the portals of the famous Queen's Elm pub. This really is a typical English tavern.

Even the barmen have plays running on Shaftesbury Avenue.
I once met a cocker spaniel that could paint, to say nothing
of a poet who could dig bigger holes in the road than anyone
else in the McAlpine outfit, but that's by the by. What is
important is the finely honed wit and badinage that issued
forth from the likes of publishers, novelists and, let's not
forget, actors. (They won't let you forget them anyway.)

By now Hans has had a busy day and as the Earls Court
Road hoves into sight he realises that all the nerve ends
inside his skull have stopped working. A quick nibble at a knot
of kebab and it's back to bed at the Shalimar Guest House.
Tomorrow could be another wonderful day and we still haven't
seen the wonders of British West Bayswater.

SHOPPING LISTS

If, in a thousand years time, sociologists and anthropologists
— let alone plain apologists — unearth the sort of shopping
list that I have to queue up behind in Lambourn then it will
probably strike them that they have unearthed the root cause
at the bottom of the decline and fall of the English 'lower
orders'. Squeamish readers are advised not to read on as other
people's tastes may cause distress, but here is the week's
intake as purchased by a deeply unattractive and averagely
rhapsodically happy woman.

It runs: 2 packets of custard creams, 6 bags of crisps, 4
large bottles of Coca-Cola, 2 tins of rice pudding, 4 Lyons
apricot fruit pies, 3 tins of evaporated milk, 1 tin each of
tangerines, peaches, pineapple slices, 2 large loaves of
sliced bread, 1 jar of lemon curd, 1 packet of Jaffa cakes, 1
packet of frozen chicken pieces, 1 lb ox heart.

After all that has been boxed up, there is a visit to the newsagent where the *Sun*, the *TV Times*, 40 Players No. 6 and an
LP of the Abba is bought. Finally, there is the call of the betting shop for a 10p yankee on Steve Cauthen's first four rides
at Bath.

Meanwhile, digging in the atomic-bomb-scorched dust

where once Old Compton Street stood, the colleagues of our Lambourn excavators may be puzzled to find a typical Saturday shopping list as carried by West End Man in the 1970s. This may puzzle them for a while until they discover a letter nearby in a mummified brief case bearing BBC letter heading.

The list comprises: 1 bottle Chianti, 1 packet of spaghetti, 1 avocado, 1 packet of Ryvita, 1 lb of strong coffee, ¼lb of Floris truffles, a sprig of fennel, 2 nectarines, 1 carton of Gitanes, a tube of instant sun tan lotion, 1 tube of KY Jelly, a copy of *Plays and Players*, a bottle of Givenchy after-shave lotion, 1 pair of silk bikini briefs, a bar of Pears soap and a Maria Callas LP.

At this point the archaeologists will think that there may have been a master race or certainly an effete species made so by malnutrition and the strain of constant creativity. Unfortunately, having stuffed and mounted Lambourn Woman and Soho Man in the Natural History Museum, a spanner will be not so much thrown in the works as dug up. This will be the result of another dig in Marylebone High Street area where the skeleton of a young woman will be found. From the *European Sunday News*, 24 June 2079.

'Scientists are investigating the body and belongings of a young woman believed to have died in the last war a thousand years ago. A shopping list consisting of ¼lb sunflower seeds, 1 lb of lentils, 6 cartons of yoghurt, ½lb bran, 2 bottles apple juice, a copy of *New Society*, the *Radio Times*, the Penguin John Donne and an LP of a Mozart Flute Concerto were found by the body. Remnants of cheesecloth clothing and some remarkably well preserved sandals were found near the body.

'Professor Brien of the Fleet Street Institute told television cameramen on the site, "What puzzles us is the fact that the poor girl was wearning no knickers when she died so suddenly. We're working on the theory that she might have been 'artistic' or what we now call insane."

'Meanwhile, more scientists are still interviewing the man found alive in a cave in the Mendips and believed to be well over a thousand years old. He was discovered by an oil prospector, Fred Robens, two days ago. Mr Robens told pressmen,

"I wandered into this cave and found him surrounded by deep freezes. He seemed quite annoyed that I'd found him. The freezes were filled with fillet steak and chocolate cake. He was surrounded by a mountain of cigarette ends and *Playboy* magazines and he had a fixed smile." Scientists are working on the theory that his longevity is due to 'happiness' or, as we call it now, insanity. Professor Brien said, "The fact that he has been left alone by sociologists for a millenium obviously hasn't done him any harm and, being in the cave when the 'big one' went up, protected him from the lethal fallout of custard creams, avocados and sunflower seeds.'''

GREEK STREET DAYS

I returned to Soho this week after 18 months of self-imposed exile to bless what is left of my pathetically sheep-like flock. Frank Blake is still descending from his flat above the Venus Club strip rooms into Maison Valerie every morning to collect his breakfast bread rolls and he's still doing it dressed in a raincoat that he thinks passes for a bath robe. In Valerie's itself the same denim-suited brigade sit about discussing the editing they're doing on their commercials and art students from St Martins come in for a coffee, inexplicably fascinated by their copies of the *Guardian*. The TV commercial boys sit there plucking their croissants and saying, 'Yes, I know love, but if we cut it there — bang, bang — like that, we wouldn't have to hold him in long shot coming down those stairs looking so dreadfully bored. Let's face it, loves, we're here, basically, to sell the wretched stuff.' 'I couldn't agree more. No, Basil's right. Cut it and let's scrap the dissolve. Incidentally, did you see Richard Three last night. My God. Of course, basically, it's a really boring play, particularly if it isn't done well, but I thought . . .' By this time my coffee was cold and my mouth locked in open-jawed disbelief.

A few minutes later, walking along Old Compton Street, I saw that the season of rifts and mellow fruitiness has improved the looks of most people and that even a couple of winos look like uncrackable walnuts and not frightened plums. In the

Swiss Tavern the dirty bookshop boys are standing around discussing last night's television documentary on Soho. 'Oh yes, lovely stuff. Reflections of neon lights in the puddles but what a load of old bollocks really.'

Around the corner in the Golden Lion a few middle-aged men look around anxiously as I poke my head through the door fearful that I might be a little richer and more handsome than they. They are waiting for sailors, guardsmen, and professional whores. They see me, realise at once that I don't represent a threat, and turn back to their gins and tonics. I move on and continue my round of the streets.

Checking up on the Carlisle Arms, a pub I haven't been in for over a year, I'm immediately tapped for £10 which is, apparently, a certainty to be returned to me at 6 pm that night in the York Minster. Bye, bye £10. Well, they say that there's no one easier to con than a con-man and I ruminate about my lost tenner in a Chinese restaurant in Gerrard Street. I never cease to be amazed at just how bloody rude and aggressive Chinese waiters are. I ask one of the owners of a duck and rice factory just why this is so and she tells me, 'You must realise that it isn't anything to do with our manner. Quite simply we hate you. I don't myself, but most waiters don't like the English and most of them are Maoist too.'

After this, there's a cocktail party and the usual embarrassment of meeting, face to face, those 'stars' that I've either teased or insulted in print somewhere or other. I notice, more and more, how extraordinarily happy people look at such functions. Why aren't they cursed with obvious anxiety? But they're not and it's all, 'Oh Christ, a really amazing film when you think that, basically, it had no plot whatsoever. I didn't like *her* but that sort of bird hasn't ever been my cup of tea. Incidentally, you know how she got discovered? She was in rep in Birmingham and this fantastic old man actually pulled her and then put her in a play that he'd basically backed.'

For the umpteenth time in six months I make a mental note to ask some bright spark like Bron Waugh to write a piece actually attacking those people who keep using the word basically when it's not necessary. Yes, that's it. That's what a return visit to London does first. It makes me think they're all talking a different language which, at this moment in time, basically, is what it's all about. I mean, I know you've got to let it all hang out and stay loose when is quite incredible and absolutely amazing in a basic sort of way, basically, that is, but it's really beginning to bug me. Basically, I'm pretty tolerant but if I go on hearing that word I think I might flip. I mean it's really draggy and, basically, out.

BLOODY SUNDAY

The old barmaid in the Lambourn Lion dished me out some very lyrical stuff the other day which set me thinking. She was talking about the good old days *v*. the present day. It's a controversy that sportsmen all too often drag out and I hope I don't have to suffer many more public-house discussions as to the comparative merits of Jack Dempsey and Muhammad Ali, Gordon Richards and Lester Piggott. The barmaid had different things in mind, which made a change. After five minutes of the desultory stuff that the first customer is usually served with she went on to say that, what with spring being around the corner, we could soon expect to be enjoying getting up and being conscious at an early hour. She enlarged on the subject.

'When I was a young girl, in the nineteen-twenties, the mornings were altogether different. We'd get up ever so early and go out to the fields to pick mushrooms and then we'd come home and cook them for breakfast which we always ate outside. In those days the mornings were always so cobwebby. You always saw beautiful cobwebs. Of course, that was before they had combine harvesters. When they used to get the harvest in in the old way the bees used to buzz. They don't buzz so much now, do they? They'd stop for lunch in the fields and cut lovely pieces of cheese with their penknives and drink cider and sometimes they'd fall asleep. It was lovely.'

All that from the mouth of Flo I found partly touching, but a bit depressing even at that early hour. A picturesque string of horses walking past the pub didn't lift the gloom and the gloom increased as I thought how even 'low life' has lost a lot of its charm. Take Saturdays. Now Saturday was always play day in London. Everyone was in town and Saturday nights nearly always ended up very happily in tears. All that stopped when, as I remember it, people took to renting, buying or staying in country cottages for the weekend. That was about twenty years ago. You could be dead in Soho on a Saturday now and hardly notice the difference.

I knew the rot had set in for sure when they knocked down the old tavern at Lords and replaced it with a lump of modern hospitality — a mess of concrete — dispensing sloppy onions and fizzy chemicals. I should have seen it coming through years before when Jack Solomons's gymnasium in Windmill Street closed down.

That really was a very rum set-up. On the first floor there was a billiard hall extraordinary and then the gym above. It was the nearest you've ever got to being in New York without the air ticket. But the billiard hall — revived in rather an anaemic way now — was something to be savoured as much as were pubs like The Highlander and Black Horse and Dog and Duck.

What made the billiard bit so odd was the complete nut-case who ran it, or at least managed it then. He looked like Boris Karloff. Not dangerous, just oddly menacing, and when I used to creep up there at 7 a.m. after a nasty night in the Corner House, he'd always greet me with bizarre and criminal insinuations.

'I'm here all alone this morning,' he'd tell me, 'and, d'you know, there must be at least £500 in the till. Just think about it. I mean it's not nice, is it? Anyone, anyone like you in fact, could walk round here, hit me over the head and take it.' I used to agree with him that it was a possibility and then he'd turn the back of his bald head on me, a head that was so rotten the freckles merged with what must have been nicotine stains that had somehow miraculously appeared with them, and I knew he was silently imploring me to mug him.

People are altogether straighter now. Only last week someone went berserk in the Helvetia and stabbed three men and the barman only said, 'Black Hussein had four stitches put in his head, Freddie got off even lighter and Mary was cut on the arm.'

Flo was right. The bees don't buzz so much any more.

3. ASPECTS OF ENGLAND: *Taki and Jeffrey Bernard*

OH, TO BE IN ENGLAND: *Taki*

Upon choosing to live under a trade union dictatorship rather than languish in a Greek gaol (it was an agonising decision) I decided to pose as an Englishman and a country squire at that.

The first thing I did was to trade in my Caraceni of Milano suits and Gucci shoes for English hand-me-downs available from the Workers Revolutionary Party benevolent fund. What I received in return was third-hand clothes — having been stolen by seething revolutionary offsprings from their parents' upper middle-class homes — but they nevertheless instantly transformed me into a pin-strip Englishman. My accent was a slight problem but I contacted my old friend Sir Charles Clore who gave me elocution lessons and taught me the public schoolboys' old trick of speaking with the mouth closed while breathing with my back. I then bought lots of back copies of *Dog* and *House*, covered my room with chintz, bought a Volvo estate wagon, installed a cage in the back of it and triumphantly drove into London. In retrospect it was the greatest mistake of my life.

Just past Baron's Court there was a road block. A policeman looked first at my car and then at my clothes and asked me what the nature of my visit to London was. He hummed and hawed for a while and finally said, 'I am terribly sorry sir, but we have allowed fifty-two people like you inside the city today. The quota is full. Please try later.' Although I was dressed like an Englishman I hardly felt like one so, pretending to obey blindly and make a U-turn, I gunned the car and drove on. Passing through Little Arabia, or the Boltons, as it used to be known, I was inundated with spittle from rich Arabs' flunkies shouting and gesticulating while waiting for their masters. Arab children riding with their nannies in Camargue Rolls-Royces jeered at me and threw precious beads.

I managed to reach Belgravia with my new-found English imperturbability still intact. Getting out to buy a newspaper I was accosted by a panhandler. 'Parakalo, parakalo,' he shouted sticking his arm out, 'drachmas, drachmas.' For a moment I thought the insidious Greeks had penetrated my disguise until I realised that all the beggars in Eaton Square were Greek-speaking Englishmen. The whole square is inhabited by Greek shipowners and even the traffic signs are in Greek. The beggars were now getting excited; 'Goulandris sahib,' they screamed, making the best of two worlds.

Some very fat Greek children were out sunning and stuffing themselves with baklava and feta sandwiches. Their prams were tanker-shaped and their English nannies wore sailor suits. Unpatriotically they laughed when the oleaginous fatty Greeks pelted me with olives and yelled 'foreigner, foreigner.'

Disheartened and disillusioned I drove on. In one of London's most famous thoroughfares, opposite the Victoria and Albert Museum, a mosque was being built. Thousands of shoes were outside it as the constructors were all Ismaili workers flown in as cheap labour. The mosque is to be a place of worship for the Ismailis whose God is Karim Aga Khan. He flies through the air with the greatest of ease in his three private jets, and cuts through the waves on his four super-yachts. Total cost over £20 million. He also has about fifteen houses and one thousand servants. Thus none of the faithful thinks he is a slob. The 'living god' wants an English mosque because both his wife and mother are English.

The sight of the mosque was the last straw. I needed a drink badly. But that proved the most difficult task of all. I dared not go into a pub dressed as a nob Englishman because I was certain to be mugged by Marxists having nothing better to do now that the polo season is over. And smart bars and restaurants would not let me enter without djellaba. 'I am sorry, sir,' was the way Louis, the elegant maître d' of Annabel's, put it. 'We are all booked for tonight and our clients do not want their seats all sweaty before they arrive.' Furious, I rang the owner, old Etonian Mark Birley. Surely he would set things right. 'Not a chance, Taki old boy,' he said, 'they won't even let me in. But do come dear boy for a hot cuppa tea.' My efforts had not been in vain. I finally understood what the old school tie network was all about.

PASTORAL: *Jeffrey Bernard*

I now realise that it's highly likely that the two biggest of many mistakes I've made were to have moved from London to Suffolk in 1966 and then again from London to Berkshire in 1978. The idea that living in the country is going to make life sheer poetry is sheer romancing — as far as I'm concerned anyway. The idyll is utterly without stimulus and all those trees and all that grass I'm sure are sprouting through, draining me. I remember once foolishly suggesting to Francis Bacon that he solve his tax problems by moving and living in Switzerland. 'Are you crazy' he said. 'All those fucking views. They'd drive me mad.'

On both the occasions I moved to the country I took a brand new wife with me. We all of us must have somehow thought that, away from the delicious low life of London, we'd be different and for the better too. Not so. We'd end up prowling around each other eyeing one another like hungry watchdogs. And the wretched pettiness that goes with roses around a cottage door is the most sickening thing of all.

Take last week, an epic week for piddling trifles. I got barred from one pub and barred myself from another. Sheer inconvenience. In the first instance I took the ex-publican of the place into a pub and the present landlord accused me of stirring it and told me not to come back. Apparently it's bad etiquette, but nonsense to my mind. In the second instance I took my daughter, her mother and step-father into my local and we asked the guvnor if he had a snack for the girl as opposed to a lunch. He was incredibly rude. 'If you want that sort of rubbish,' he said, 'then you should go to the service station on the motorway.' Added to that he refused me chips with a piece of fish (necessary, after a jab of insulin), saying, 'It isn't on the bloody menu.'

As I say, very petty stuff and just about too petty to even report. But it's just about the last straw and this camel's back is cracking. As for writing one's wretched 'novel' in the peace and quiet of the country — forget it. The loneliness and the shattering silence drive me to the pubs run by these jumped-up shopkeepers and although that's my own inadequacy it's still a fact. Now, I'm running out of pubs, small talk and the patience to pass the time of day with people who can see no further than the end of their wretched lane. To spend — as I do sometimes in London — an hour in the company of the likes of Tom Baker, journalistic colleagues, female company — non-existent in the sticks — is to wallow in the luxury of being alive. That awesome feeling and terrifying presence that can overwhelm you in a wood or forest is the life force that saps you down here. Me, anyway.

COUNTRY STYLE: *Taki*

Whenever the subject of living in the country as opposed to living in the city came up, my old friend the seventh Earl of Lucan would get furious. 'Lucky' could not understand how people who did not have to chose to go there during weekends. 'Only savages live in the bush,' he would say, 'Or Aspers, who likes wild animals and has a death wish.'

During those halcyon days when Lucan was still around as well as Dominic Elwes, and Charles Benson had not yet become a member of the royal family, I had a flat in Mayfair. It was very convenient because I could roll out of bed and be at Aspinall's and gambling in exactly three minutes flat if I really was pushed. And I usually was. Gambling is more difficult to shake than heroin and in those days I was really hooked. A daily fix of chemmy was something I could not go without.

When Aspinall sold his club to the Playboy Club and left the country things changed. Lucan got so upset that he made one of the greatest gaffes of mistaken identity I know. Dominic Elwes couldn't take it any longer and simply killed himself, and Charles Benson went further than any of us; he got married and began hanging around with royals. Worse, he would leave every weekend for the country. I, being more stable than the English, did not over-react. Shrewdly I bided my time and when Aspinall opened a club in Sloane Street I moved all the way to what Lucan called the outskirts of Heathrow. In fact the last time I talked to him he warned me about getting hit by a low-flying plane. 'Tregunter Road, Cathcart and The Boltons are as dangerous as living down here,' he screamed over the field phone he used to contact me. 'Make sure you sleep in the basement, old chum.'

Although I still think that Lucan and I were right in considering anything west of Sloane Square to be the countryside, I decided to move out of the city and into SW10 for personal reasons. First of all, I can now write in peace. Also, the milk and vegetables are fresher, and it's easier to cut a wide swath through the Tregunter set of Third World socialites and potential future queens. But it also has its drawbacks; like becoming too adventurous and taking oneself for an explorer. This is what I did last weekend.

Although my pith helmet, mosquito net and snake repellent guaranteed my survival in the wild northern countryside of Leicestershire, it did nothing to protect me from the mores and manners of country gentry. There was the matter of dress. I must admit I felt a bit of a fool as I spent all weekend dressed up in tails and white tie while my host and some other vulgarians walked around in jeans. No one had bothered to tell me that, unlike the Greeks, who dress for their weekends in Vouliagmeni, the English have degenerated to such an extent that they don't even wear tails at dinner. The butler, however, a cousin and namesake of the Foreign Minister, was dressed like me though he had an extra layer of brown Derbyshire soup.

Then there was the fun and games, if one can call it that. One of the guests, an art dealer and croquet hustler who looks like Art Garfunkel, displayed what he called a Hurlingham grip that was so indecent that some of the ladies left. Nicholas Soames, Winston Churchill's grandson and the only member of the family who might follow the great man's footsteps due to his uncanny ability to insult people, was another guest. Soames is a very talented young man having been an equerry to Prince Charles; he has also stood as a Tory candidate in a staunch left-wing constituency and survived, as well as having advised Sir James Goldsmith on his way to the top. But tennis is not his forte. Naturally, I was paired with him against a young, buxom, horse-fancying blonde and a fading old commodity broker who used to be my fag at Eton. The result was more humiliation for me as Soames, although calling the lines like an Italian, managed to hit me more times than he did the other end of the court.

But it was the riveting conversation that ensured the fact that I shall never return to the country. It ranged from fertilising, to goats, to sex, back to fertilising, more goats, sex, horses and the forthcoming grouse season. It usually ended with a wild symphony of farts, belches and loud laughter. Needless to say, the worst humiliation was left until the end. Soames warned me that being a foreigner and in the house for the first time I was expected to give a £1,000 tip to the butler. This I did. As I drove away I looked in the back of the stables; there were the guests, laughing wildly, belching, and spliting my tip among them.

COLD COMFORT: *Jeffrey Bernard*

There's a damp, still greyness in the country in January which, combined with the cold, makes me bury my head for half the day in the railway timetable to see what time the next train to London departs Newbury. The trouble is I know exactly what's going on in London so that a trip there would be a case of jumping out of the fridge and into the ice bucket. It's as it always is but with overcoats on. But, down here, I think the winter's killing everyone. It's as though no one cares anymore. They've given up. They can't be bothered to wipe those red and dripping noses. The conversational record has got stuck in a groove and I don't think it would be a bad idea if it were made a criminal offence to wish people a happy New Year after 7 January.

Yesterday I went into one of my locals at midday for an aperitif and the barmaid was still hoovering the floor. They'd run out of tonics, forgotten to put the soup on, were short of change for the cigarette machine and an idiot in the public bar kept playing the same dreadful record on the juke box over and over again. And they wonder why Burgess, Maclean and Philby made such a close study of the continental time-tables.

It was while I was reflecting on these matters that the Backbone of England and his wife came into the bar. These people invariably make the same entrance wherever they go and I presume they are rehearsed in it as children. She, in her sheepskin coat and headscarf, said 'Brrrr'. He, in his anorak, clapped his hands together several times and then rubbed them vigorously together. 'What'll you have, darling?' he said. 'Ooh, let's see. What shall I have?' I was rivetted immediately. 'Why don't you have a whisky mac, darling?' 'Yes, why don't I have a whisky mac? Good idea, darling. Right, I'll have a whisky mac. What are you going to have, darling?' 'Ooh, I'm not sure, darling. I know, I think I'll have a nice bottle of Guinness.' I just managed to suppress a scream. He reached into his pocket for some money, dropped a coin on the floor and the hoover-operator said, 'Leave it for the sweeper'. Minutes later, when they had all three of them recovered from the witticism and the drinks had been served, the Backbones of England smiled lovingly and knowingly at each other, took a long look around the bar and then he said to the barmaid, 'Busy Christmas?' 'Ooh, terrible. Packed all the time we were.' 'Well,' said the Backbone, 'that's over for another year, anyway.' Their three noses dripped once in unison and then Mrs Backbone decided it was time for her to scintillate. 'Yes,' she said, 'that's over for another year, isn't it, darling?' 'Yes,' he said, nodding approvingly at a horse-brass, 'that's all over.'

While this was going on I stared gloomily ahead at a row of

bottles, terrified that I might be dragged into the badinage. (It's always good protection against the Backbones to look miserable.) I knew, deep down, that they were going to continue to plunder the calendar and I waited for it, like a man who knows he's about to be hurt by a clumsy doctor. Sure enough, Mr Backbone put down his drink, rubbed his hands together and asked the Still Life with Hoover, 'How was the New Year then?' 'New Year?' she asked, indignantly. 'Don't talk.' 'Oh, like that was it?' laughed Backbone. 'Like that, eh?' echoed Mrs Backbone. The barmaid grunted. 'Ours was pretty hectic too, wasn't it, darling?' 'Always is. Still, you expect it to be, don't you?' 'Wouldn't be New Year if it wasn't, would it, darling? Shall we have another? Just one teensy-weensy one, darling?' 'Why not?' The three of them roared with laughter, sputtered to a stop and then sniffed. I left before they embarked on forecasts for Easter.

Across the road at the garage, old Pop was rubbing his hands together. He looked up at me as I walked in and said 'Brrr'. I asked him if he'd got a taxi that could take me to Newbury Station. He said, No, his daughter didn't do it anymore now that she was married and even if she hadn't been married he doubted whether she would have in this cold weather. Then he gave me another 'Brrrr' and I left.

When I got home the stove had gone out and that takes a wretched hour to clear out and get going again. I went out to the paddock where they dump the logs and Horace the pony was chewing one of them. He looked up at me and snorted. It's a funny noise when a horse blows out air. It sounds just like 'Brrrr'.

4. SKATING ON THIN ICE: *Jeffrey Bernard*

FACE LIFTS

It's always nice to stay in a house where they put Malvern Water, *Vogue* and a bowl of fruit on the bedside table. It makes such a change from an infused tea bag, the *Racehorse* and a limp biscuit. It was delightful to be able to sit up in some-one else's bed last week listening to the servants pottering about downstairs and to read *Health and Slimming Vogue* and discover how the beautiful people make themselves beautiful. The article which really grabbed me was one that disclosed what various well known women do to their faces and what they do to keep their shape. *Vogue*, I think, must be read by people completely and utterly out of touch with reality, but it's good for a laugh. I mean, would you believe what Antonia Fraser does to herself?

She puts on Miss Dior Eau de Toilette as soon as she gets up and uses the perfume later in the day. She goes to John of Thurloe Place once a week to have her hair washed because it's so peaceful reading a book under the drier. She uses Elizabeth Arden Visible Difference just before her evening bath which always has Mary Chess Gardenia Foam in it. Furthermore, she couldn't live without wholemeal bread from Cranks with Cooper's Oxford marmalade for breakfast and she likes Revlon Natural Wonder All Weather Pink Lip Moisturiser and Clinique Glossy Brush-on Mascara and a little bit of silvery blue eyeshadow.

Amazing, isn't it? She probably dusts her typewriter with Floris Talcum Powder and writes on rice paper that's been sprayed with rose water, pausing at 11 a.m. to nibble on a truffle that's been washed in Femme Eau de Cologne. It all makes me wonder if there's anything you couldn't do in this life if you cherished yourself as much as that. Bette Davis, on the other hand, has honed down the self-coddling to a bare minimum. 'My beauty secret,' she says, 'is to eat only half of what is on my plate and not drink at lunchtime.' I suppose she must order large portions and drink at breakfast time.

My own beauty secrets are somewhere half-way between those of Miss Davis and the great biographer. As soon as I wake up I smoke three or four Senior Service and then cough for ten minutes. I like to cough into Kleenex For Men Tissues which I buy chez Packwood of Lambourn. Then I get up and make the first cup of tea with a Marks & Spencer teabag. I usually go back to bed for 20 minutes and study the day's runners and riders while my wife strokes my forehead and begs me to pull myself together. When I get up I wash in water, if the pipes haven't frozen and burst. I'm very fond of Thames Water Board water which we have specially piped in.

Twice a week I wash my hair in Head and Shoulders but if I'm in London I go to Greek Chris of Aldo's in Old Compton Street. I like to relax with his old copies of *Men Only* and *Penthouse* while he blow-dries my hair; if I have to wait I relax by playing gin rummy with Italian Albert. Incidentally, like Antonia Fraser, I'm an absolute stickler for a healthy breakfast. I usually fry up some bubble and squeak with half a pound of Newmarket sausages, two eggs, three rashers of bacon and some baked beans. After breakfast I answer the threatening letters and drink a litre of Charbonnier Red Table Wine shipped and bottled by R. & C. Vitners, Carrow, Norwich. I find this gives my skin a healthy pink glow and it helps to keep my eyes open. I have to be very careful of my weight and so often go without lunch although I do sometimes weaken and have a packet of Smith's Crisps with my vodka, lime and soda.

I am particularly fussy about my clothes as well as my skin and figure, as anyone short of money has to be. One must keep up appearances and since my novel is not selling well — possibly because it hasn't been written — I do like to give the impression that all is not yet quite lost. For my foundation garments I go to Marks & Spencer who sell particularly restrictive briefs, making a vasectomy quite unnecessary. I get my suits off the peg but for special occasions I buy trousers from Paul of Berwick Street who was at one time by appointment to the late George Formby and Jack Spot. Sleep is important to morning freshness and I take two valium with a mug of Ovaltine and whisky before burying my face in my pillow and sobbing myself to sleep.

HARD LINES

I sat opposite an Indian tramp on a tube train the other day — the first *Indian* tramp I've ever seen — and he looked to be in very bad shape indeed. He was twitching with what I guess was some sort of malnutritional ailment and he was in need of all sorts of help. After a few minutes, I got to the end of my cigarette, dropped it onto the floor and put it out with my foot. A second too late, the tramp bent down to rescue it from being crushed. The other passengers in that part of the carriage suddenly became aware of the little scene and I too, suddenly, was overwhelmed by a feeling of embarrassment. What I should have done was to give the man a cigarette but I didn't because I suppose that in the back of my mind I thought I'd be regarded as being eccentric by the other passengers. The point is, I despise myself for the thought. The episode was over in five seconds and you may think it a pretty trivial business, but I should have given the man a cigarette, and a lousy pound note wouldn't have done either him or me any harm. The timing of the incident — my foot getting to the cigarette a split second before his hand — made it look so cruel.

'So what?' you may ask, but I think quite frequently of tramps, drop-outs and winos and that's because I don't think they're *that* far removed from the rest of us. The fact that I got to know so many such men when I did my three-month stint in an alcohol and drug addiction unit at one time makes me a trifle more sympathetic toward them than most people, but I'm not calling on you to get out your gipsy violins. I'm simply saying that if you can understand people cracking in action at war you must understand that people can crack in deathless peace. Anyway, one shouldn't be frightened of giving someone a cigarette. But it's made me reflect on the pros and cons of dropping out.

I considered it quite seriously at one time when I was deeply depressed but in the end I had to reject it on purely practical and materialistic grounds. Drop-outs don't have clean sheets, let alone beds, they can't wallow in hot baths studying the *Sporting Life* and it's extremely unlikely that they ever get anyone to bed. Admittedly, after a while on the streets, sexual desire must go down the drain alongside the desire to work and live normally. But what if it doesn't? Then, of course, those long lunches bathed in claret would be absent. Then there's the cold, and God knows how many tramps must snuff it during the winter months.

But what is odd, and that strikes me as being something of a paradox, is the fact that your average tramp just hasn't been equipped for such a hard life. The survival kit for managing on crusts, meths and the fag end round a fire on a bombed site is a public school background. Anyone who went to a public school say 30 years ago — I assume they've improved beyond recognition by now — could certainly live on fairly disgusting food as could anyone who went to a particularly nasty camp for their National Service. I'm sure it's well nigh impossible to be wetter or colder than I was at the very first Outward Bound which was at Aberdovey, but I don't think I could take another 15 years of celibacy like the stretch I served between 1932 and 1947.

But when it all goes wrong, when the buff envelopes pile up and when the envy keeps creeping up like bile and all I can say is 'fuck it', then I do tend to regard the hot-air-ventilated pavement grills outside bakers' shops as possible beds. As I say though, they must be fearfully hard to entertain on. Dinner for two on the pavement above the Regent Palace kitchen? 'Sorry, we're full up mate. No room.' Lunch on the never ending trip around the Inner Circle? 'Tickets please.' Actually, I bet there's some nutty lady somewhere who'd say yes.

BLISS

There was a harmless spread in last week's *Daily Express* which caught my eye and then summoned my gall which was headed 'TRUE HAPPINESS IS . . .' and subtitled, 'a heart-warming guide to life's most rewarding emotions from the famous and not so famous'. It was pretty predictable stuff and I quote the offering from Harry Secombe. 'Happiness is the crisply folded, unread newspaper; the smell of bacon frying first thing in the morning. It is the sound of children singing hymns and the feeling of satisfaction after a job well done. The knowledge that you are loved for what you are, and not for what you pretend to be. But above all, happiness is having my wife and children around me, and my grand-daughter on my knee.'

I like it. Lovely stuff. Unfortunately for me not one of Mr Secombe's items applies at the moment. The crisply folded, unread newspaper will remain unread until I've paid the newsagent's bill and the smell of bacon frying first thing in the morning as I grope blindly for a cigarette and drown in remorse is enough to make me vomit. Now, the sound of children singing hymns serves only to remind me of the fearful thrashing I received at school when, as a member of the choir, I organised a futile strike for the choir to have an extra day's holiday at half term. As for the knowledge that I might be loved for what I am and not for what I pretend to be I'm afraid I don't really know what he's talking about. I don't *pretend* to be anything. If someone loves me then it's they who are pretending. I'm someone and something else. As for having one's wife and children surround one, which particular wife is he talking about? Of course, the grandchild on the knee is completely out of the question. Someone else's grandchild sat on my knee only this morning and within minutes I was covered in snot and strawberry jam.

I think I prefer the Duke of Westminster's effort to listen to balms, the balms of life. In spite of the fact that he should have simply said, 'happiness is being the Duke of West-minster,' the young whipper-snapper said, 'being alone with my wife in the privacy of our own home is something I value

above all.' I should bloody well think so too. I for one wouldn't
mind (a) being alone in his home, (b) being alone with the
Duchess of Westminster in his home, (c) being alone with the
Duchess of Westminster in my own home. In actual fact I
don't think I'd mind being the Duchess of Westminster
herself, never mind the Duke.

But what is this nonsense of happiness itself being available to all and sundry like a loaf of bread or a pint of milk?
What on earth makes people think that they have the *right* to
be happy? Why can't people get it through their heads that
life, by and large, is pretty bloody boring and that the good
days are the exception and not the rule. D'you remember
Patience Strong? It always amazed and invariably amused me
that she used to write in her column that she could be happy
at the drop of a hat. Well, if not at the drop of a hat then at the
sound of the patter of tiny feet, a blackbird singing in the
garden in the morning or the sight of a red rose. Haven't
these people anything to *think* about?

The last time I heard the patter of feet — admittedly not
exactly tiny — was when I backed a two-year-old which came
in a remote seventh. As for roses, they serve to remind me of
the last person I sent some to. I've been pondering just what
trifles do make me happy and it's hard to come up with a
trifling list.

I suppose, the post without a buff-coloured envelope. A
benign magistrate. A comparatively silent barmaid. Flattery.
Kissing the girls and making them cry. The optimism of
publishers. Being with people with a sense of the absurd.
Deluding myself that, starting tomorrow it's all going to be
different. Skating on thin ice and surviving.

SANS TEETH

Every time I go to Newbury I hear bad news. The place is
becoming a veritable slough of despond. Last month, The
Chequers put up the price of a very moderate glass of wine
to an exorbitant 60p. At the last race meeting, Fred Binns
told me I still owed him £20 from Ascot, and last week a

cheery Australian looked into my mouth and told me he'd have to take out all my top teeth on 20 March. This last in a series of nasty psychological shocks is very nearly the last straw and I reckon that if I can't do something soon about my persistent dandruff then my hair will be coming out in sympathy. When I think what my body and I have gone through over the past 45 years I should have thought it might have the decency to hang on a little longer — at least until the hot weather started. It is not a pretty sight.

Starting at the top the memory banks are now completely empty, the concentration fuses have blown and only a few basic animal instincts remain. Fleeting moments of lust and greed occasionally threaten to turn the motor over but the spark is weak. Just below that dusty attic two pink eyes peer out betraying the absence of any constructive thought. The nose drips from early September until the Newmarket meeting in April and the mouth, soon to be half empty, is half open and tells its own sordid tale.

I read somewhere recently that the eyes reveal the present, the mouth the past and the line of the chin what was given in the beginning. If it's true it's an unnerving thought for those of us with chins showing all the determination of a pudding. Below the frightened chin the skin on the neck, like the rings in a tree trunk, tells the time of life and a stock of roll-neck jerseys is essential camouflage.

I now sit glued to the television set taking an alarmingly new and keen interest in commercials for denture fixatives. How can I be sure they really work? When will they fail? I know when. On the 18.30 from Paddington to Newbury. Sometimes I take a nap on that train after an exhausting and investigative day in London and when I doze off the plate will slowly slip. By Reading it will be half way out and in my lap by Thatcham. I'll awake to the sneering stares of a carriage full of businessmen. Or, of course, it could well happen at a party and at the inevitable moment when I'm trying to impress and flirt.

Toothless friends and acquaintances tell me there's nothing to it like so many Mother Hubbards talking of childbirth, but I don't believe it. The Newbury Australian wasn't exactly

reassuring about things either. Did I bleed easily when I cut,
he asked me? Would I be accompanied by my next of kin
when the job is done? It occurred to me then that my next-of-
kin, dear thing that she is, might well never want to set eyes
on me again. But it could, I suppose, be worse. A doctor could
have told me, 'Six months, I'm afraid. Possibly a year,' and I
saw just that happen to Robert Donat in a film the other day.
It did wonders for him and even had me reaching for a handkerchief. He suddenly saw what's called the light. For the rest
of the film he was plunged into a sort of facuous serenity. He
couldn't stop smiling at everyone though, of course, he did
have his teeth. He became like the Irishman who thought
that where you go when you die must be a great place since
no one's ever come back from it.

I will now stop moaning and attempt to 'do' a Robert Donat.
I will go from hence and pat small children on the head. I will
find the money somehow to send my daughter to the Royal
College of Music, or what she will. At the end of the month, if
you do happen to see a man being arrested on platform 1 at
Newbury and lisping to the police, it will be me.

ANOTHER AMAZING FIND

It was just two weeks after the discovery of the Byron letters in
the Pall Mall branch of Barclays Bank that I made my own
startling find. There in a carrier bag, stuffed under my bed,
I found a wodge of letters written to me during the past three
years. They have yet to be edited, but a random selection gives
some idea of the richness of the find, whose value has already
been estimated at three pounds.

Dear Jeffrey

A brief note that I can find time to write while Paddy is out
at the pub getting more money back on the empties. Jesus and
Mary, mother of God, how I wish I'd never come to this
country in the first place. Not that I'd change the knowing of
you for all the agonies of my own childhood, or at least the
memory of it, by returning to the arid hell of the Connemara
hills and all they meant to me and my mother as well as the

grey pain of all the unfulfilment in Dublin itself; no, it's not
that, my treasure, and I can call you that knowing that you
love Doris Lessing more than I, it's simply — or is it perhaps
difficulty — that the surfeit of everything black and sad about
Dublin and what was lacking there for me, at any rate, is
my love for you and the gigantic desire that I have to write
another bestseller. We will, I know, meet at another
publisher's cocktail party soon. Until then, my Celtic love to
you and hush your guilt.

Love, Edna

That letter from Edna O'Brien is fairly typical of the sort of
missile I was receiving after my divorce four years ago. But
my first post-marital correspondents were by no means all
women, as this letter from my psychiatrist, Dr Benno Brendel,
proves.

Dear Mr Bernard

It is with regret that I notice that you have cancelled or failed
to turn up for your last six appointments. I am beginning to
wonder, are you confusing love with money? The last time
you were here, you may remember that we discussed, at some
length, your attitude towards women and your reluctance to
pay for your mother's funeral which, I believe I am right in
saying, took place some thirty years ago.

You now owe me sixty pounds and while I am fully aware
that your guilt was the problem we were working on I learn
from another patient of mine, a charming gentleman from
North London, that you owe your bookmaker no less than
£564. Is your guilt, perhaps, an enormous fantasy? Deliberate
on this, write down all your anxiety dreams and please come
and see me next Tuesday at 11 a.m.

Yours sincerely, Benno Brendel

It was shortly after I received that letter that I was plunged
into the depths of despair by the death of my dog Coxswain.
Returning to my club, the Colony Room in Dean Street, after
the funeral at Six Yard Bottom, I was to learn, much to my joy,
that I had at least one friend.

Dear Jeff

Intrinsically, you don't have to tell me. Basically, I was
brought up with animals. I know, and with regard to this one I

really mean it, what it's like to lose something steeped in clay — you could call it the earth — that's to say something that evokes childhood and all that's natural and simple and good. What I'm trying to say, and it probably isn't going to help, is if it would relieve the pain in any way, would you like to come on my new programme, 'Read Any Good Books Latterly?' The Beeb are giving me £700 a week for doing it and we're paying guests on the show two pounds an appearance. Think about it and if you fancy the idea, do come along.

Yours, Melvyn

Only two days passed after that reassuring letter from Melvyn Bragg when I was brought sharply and painfully down to earth again.

Dear Mr Bernard

It is with some regret that the Austro-Anglian Laundry learn that you have omitted to pay your bills for the past six months. Your account at the moment stands at forty-three pounds and seventy-six pence. Remittance would oblige.

Yours faithfully, [signature illegible]

I include this trivial and banal letter simply because it marked a turning point in my life. It was, you might say, the last straw. It made me more determined than ever to go into voluntary exile or, if you prefer it, to change address to avoid my creditors. The next day I bade farewell to my old friends Margaret Drabble, André Previn, Antonia Fraser and Russell Harty and moved to Marylebone High Street. It was there that I was to suffer the first postal heartache of my self-imposed exile.

Dear Jeffrey

It was madness from the start. You must have known as well as I that it could never work. Why on earth did we ever start it? Your moods crushed me. I put out a hand, but you never took it. Well, you did take. My God, that's all you ever did. Take, take, take. You say you like women, but I really think you hate them. Not once did you ever listen to me when I talked about me. You were just waiting for me to stop talking and get my clothes off. Then, in the Chinese restaurant in Gerrard Street, you finally did it. You insulted everything I hold sacred. The family unit, Carshalton Beeches, *Cosmo-*

politan and money. No, I'm sorry, it's all over. I hope you find true happiness, as I have with a property developer from Mayfair.

Juliet

Blinded by tears and fury I embarked on a series of unsatis-factory and enviable one-night stands. After six months of this mode of life, made even more harsh by a self-imposed diet of Pernod and digestive biscuits, I struck up a correspondence with one of the most brilliant novelists of her day, Andrea Newman.

Darling,

We're so busy rehearsing my new series I've had to snatch a moment in the BBC canteen to write to you. The first fifty episodes of 'Life is a Bunch of Landmines' have gone down frightfully well and there's a chance they'll be serialised by *Honey*. But that's not why I'm writing to you. I'm writing to enclose something that came to me in the middle of the night when I turned to find you gone.

There are some who say you're a shit
But I know that there's just a little bit
Of what makes the world go round.
That's love and not the falling pound.
I know that life is not a bowl of cherries
But one long case of clap and beri-beri
So give it one more chance my love
And come and live with me in Hove.

Love, Andrea

Needless to say, there are hundreds of other letters, notes and bills, but to give you some idea of the harshness of the life of a writer in exile I reproduce a letter that, for me, sums up the agony that was yesteryear. I had just completed the seventy-sixth verse of my epic canto 'Casanova' when this came tumbling through the letter box:

Dear Mr Bernard

I read with interest your letter in the *New Statesman* asking for details of your whereabouts between 1964 and 1972.

On a certain night in September 1969 you telephoned my mother to inform her that you were going to murder her only son.

I can put you in touch with several other people who have had similar bizarre and interesting experiences in your company.

Yours faithfully, Michael Molloy

Editor, *Daily Mirror*, London EC4

MONEY MATTERS

It seems strangely apposite that on the day I was asked to turn my attention to the 'low life' I should be informed by post that there was a warrant out for my arrest. What is a little more than a nuisance is that I should incur the only debt a man can be imprisoned for except for non-payment of rates. Now, like the drowning man whose past floats before his eyes, I find myself reflecting on just how I got into this mess. Incidentally, I don't for one minute believe that a drowning man hears the school bell ring for prep, the bell ring for last orders or the church bell ring for his wedding. I believe that a drowning man thinks, 'Christ almighty, I'm drowning.' But that's by the by and I'll report more fully on the subject after I have very nearly drowned which I probably will at some point. Anyway, what was I saying? Yes, how did I get into this mess?

Well for one thing I can't entirely discount hereditary factors. My mother wasn't just an opera singer, she was a positive prima donna of the county courts. One of my most treasured memories of her is of a stunning performance she gave during the war when she appeared in court for failing to keep up with a hire-purchase order. She'd got something in the Sheraton or Chippendale line — she thought big but daintily — and owed payments. In a verbal slanging match with the prosecuting counsel she was well ahead on points when the judge interrupted to tell her, 'If you continue to speak like that, Mrs Bernard, I shall have to commit you for contempt of court.' She directed her attention to him and replied, 'Make it *utter* contempt.' After the applause had died down the judge ordered her to pay a monthly mite.

I'm afraid I shall have no such luck. For one thing I haven't inherited my mother's élan. Just her ability to skate on thin ice and now that's worn a bit too thin. What I can say here though, which I'd be hard put to explain to a judge in court, is that a preoccupation with and affection for the low life is something that involves quite ridiculous economics. You'd be amazed at just how much the downhill struggle costs. A first class single to the gutter nowadays is a minimum of £10,000 a year and that's without paying tax, rates, telephone, electricity, gas and all the unnecessary essentials like clothing and food.

I suppose that in some ways I'm paying the price for choosing my friends wisely. There are no bank managers, area managers, solicitors, army officers or stockbrokers in my belt and most of my acquaintances would agree that Hamlet hit the nail on the head when he inquired as to who would bear fardels. The fardels borne by an average family in Haslemere such as life insurance, BUPA contributions, annual holidays in the Algarve plus weekly contributions to Tesco and the local Christmas club eat away at the ammunition one needs to lead a double life and yet *they* seem to pay up with little effort. The law is kind to the exception that does fall by the wayside and you might have noticed that when a man who loves the middle life goes broke for thousands he invokes little more than murmurs of sympathy from the bench. Go bust for £325.89 though and there's all sorts of trouble. What gets up the law's nose is how you go broke.

It's one thing to ask for an overdraft to buy five hundred begonias for the borders in Haslemere but quite another to seek financial succour to avail oneself of some of the 5-2 they're offering on Ile de Bourbon for the St Leger. I can't see that one is necessarily more magnificent than the other unless, of course, you knock the gardener who's planting the begonias for his wages. But, I must stress, I'm not complaining. I plotted a course for the county court and I've arrived at my destination having cunningly avoided the rocks of Haslemere, the quicksands of Wimbledon and the shoals of Bournemouth. It remains to be seen whether I shall be allowed pen and paper to address you from Brixton or whether the court will believe that, starting tomorrow, it's all going to be different.

LIFE SWAP

To begin with I felt flattered at the suggestion that Taki and I should swap columns if not places. For a moment there I felt like a Sugar Ray Robinson late flourish and was reminded of the sudden reversal of form that can come about when a champion's back touches the ropes. That and the old boxing adage that class always tells in the end.

But it wouldn't do, you know. Apart from the paradox that you meet a better class of person in low life than you do in the high variety, I simply couldn't go to all that boring trouble and expense to step into Taki's Gucci shoes.

The trappings and the paraphernalia I'd have to acquire make a pretty silly shopping list. Two dinner jackets — one white and one black — skiing equipment, a chemically induced suntan, membership of Regine's in Paris, Annabel's and Tramps in London, a course in disco dancing at the Arthur Murray school, a pilot's licence, a Panamanian passport, an elephantine tolerance to Sloane and St Moritz rangers and — impossible without an adoption certificate — a rich father and/or mother.

As it is, the equipment needed to be a low life correspondent comprises one pair of jeans and a jersey, one suit, shirt and tie for court and racetrack appearances, a wristwatch to tell me when I've outworn my welcome, a packed lunch and the goodwill of a bank manager, bookmaker, publican and wife. As for winter sports, no equipment is needed for skating on thin ice: I am already a member of the Colony Room Club in Dean Street, La Cave in Gerrard Street, Richard Ingrams's cricket team and the diabetic clinic at the Royal Free.

I'd feel even more uneasy about the swapping of friends than I would columns and, on the same score, I'm sure Taki would be like an olive out of a Martini. I may be wrong but I doubt his ability to savour the ignorance, bad taste, vacuity and frightened togetherness of some of my best friends. You may be able, as I am, to imagine me driving a Ferrari, but can you imagine Taki catching the 106 bus from Newbury to Lambourn loaded down with 6 lbs of potatoes and two deck-chairs newly obtained on credit and carrying a truly cherished bus time-table? I don't think it's on.

Then of course, the one thing I'd have to own eventually to missing is that very discomfort, anxiety and penury that keeps us low-lifers on our toes. To wake up as I imagine Taki does with no bigger challenge to face all day than a lunch with Bianca Jagger, a shirt-fitting at Turnbull & Asser and a charge account at the Cavalry Club must indeed be soporific. To run with the fox is far more invigorating than hunting with the hounds. There may be no thanksgiving service for us at the end of the day but we sleep sweetly knowing that tomorrow will very likely be far worse than today.

No, I often feel sorry for the likes of Taki. Fancy backing a winner and only having the satisfaction that you're right, not even appreciating the loot. Imagine the infinite variety of things his custom must stale. How he must crave cod and chips after making a meal of caviare. I can see him now dining in the Mirabelle, a ravishing beauty opposite eating out of his hand and him knowing he's on a winner. But can he, like me, look back on those pioneering days when seduction was like the conquest of Everest, a Chinese takeaway and up four flights to a grotty bed-sitter with an old boot and dodging the ever hungry landlady on the way?

And what is he like in a tight corner? What good could his karate expertise do him when trapped in a tight corner of the French Pub? Suppose Alan Brien came in one door and threatened him with a monologue while a *Cosmopolitan* writer, a *Guardian* Woman's Page journalist and an investigative *Observer* hack came through the other promising to drop names on him, lash him with feminist scorn and deafen him with self-congratulatory prattle? He couldn't get out of that. No, Taki is better equipped to take the high road. I'll take the low one.

5. LIVING WELL IS THE BEST REVENGE: *Taki*

LIVING WELL

In the summer of 1956 I had the bad luck to go to Greece and for once play well during the Greek national tennis tournament. I say bad luck because if I had simply gone to bed at dawn as was — and is my custom — my life might have turned out different. But that summer I was feeling not myself and I trained hard. Thus when I failed to get knocked out after the first round, I fell for the hyperbole of Greek arse-lickers who decided right then and there that I was about to win Wimbledon.

The rest is easy to guess. I returned to University, but as they say, how can you keep them down on the farm once they have seen Paris? I knew that I could go on the tennis circuit and be totally free, so why bother with an education. After all, most of the people I had met until then could only count, but were unable to read or write. (In fact Niarchos could count up to two thousand million.) And I knew how to count up to one hundred million. My father, however, did not agree. He told me I had two choices. Continue at university, or work on one of his ships or factories. I took the easy way out, ran away from home and went to Florida. Once there I began hustling tennis.

My fascination with the rich began in Palm Beach. The rich would look good while hitting the ball, but would never sweat. Nor would they try too hard, no matter how much money we had wagered, or what handicap they had received. On the other hand, whenever I played someone poor, things were

different. The poor would run all over the place and kill themselves to win the few dollars we had bet. Right then and there
I decided the rich were more fun, as well as easier to get
along with.

After a while my father decided that having a son who was
no good except at tennis was better than having a son who had
clipped every rich man south of the Mason-Dixon line, and
asked me to come home. He provided me with a small income
which was to grow larger as I grew older. Having had a taste
of fun and games, I accepted. Thus I began a long string of
parties that started in Gstaad during the winter, went on to
Paris and London during the spring, continued onto the
Riviera during the summer, Greece in the autumn, and
culminated in New York when the winter set in.

It was a fun life while it lasted. I married a beautiful
countess who also didn't know how to read or write, and saw
only people who could count. Despite their handicap, however,
most night-club characters had something more to them than
just their zest for nightlife. There was nothing sad about them,
and soon most noctambules become philosophers. It was just
about that time — during the sixties — that the really rich
stopped going out, what with terrorists and paparazos all over
the place. The people who continued to drink and dissipate,
and self-destruct were no different than the people Jeffrey
Bernard writes about. They just went to more expensive
places. *C'est tout*. My Rubirosa, Capuro, Pignatari, Herrera,
Sweeny, Zographos, Hemingway, Beer, Washer,
D'Arcangues, Miguens, and Soldati, were no different than
his crowd. Some of them were poets, like Capuro, others were
lovers, like Rubi. Most of them died driving home from a
party. The main point was that none of us — like Bernard's
friends — wanted a nine to five job. I have always insisted that
it takes an idiot or a very limited person to hold a regular job
if he can possibly help it.

Nevertheless, after the great equaliser, the welfare state,
made it possible for everyone to hang out at Annabel's, I
decided to ditch wife, friends, and familiar places, and become
an intellectual. I went to Vietnam to get an education. And I
returned more convinced than ever that the most brutal of

hoaxes was socialism. (Socialists the world over were against US involvement there, but socialists the world over have suddenly lost their voice when it comes to the greatest crime against humanity ever perpetrated since the Gulag. Both in Vietnam and in Cambodia.)

The only way one can hurt phoney socialists, and I don't know any real ones, is to live well. They say that living well is the best revenge. Well, I have been having it since 1973 to be exact. That is when I began living well again, and at times even hanging around people who can read and write. I still go to Gstaad, still hang around Annabel's every night, still have a yacht, still pursue the weaker sex with vigour, but with a purpose. At the end of the week I spill the beans on the pages of the *Spectator*, *Esquire*, and numerous other publications not important enough to mention. I have found the perfect outlet for my writing. As I always hated the rich who are known only for being rich, I twit their nose week in, week out. And sometimes I even remind the few people who read me that even the rich are better than those whores who for years apologised for the Soviet regime, and who now try to undermine the free enterprise system by pretending that there is a better way. Sometimes, I too, wish that I could be totally carefree, worry only about the rent and telephone, and not about encroaching socialism, the double standard of Marxists, and the fact that most left-wingers are prone to love the high life much more than the low life. But after a while I come back to reality. I would love to have Jeffrey's freedom but I wouldn't want to hang around with people who don't treasure it as much as I do.

VENGEFUL

There is a mordant Spanish proverb which says that living well is the best revenge. While cruising the Ionian sea on board a fully air-conditioned 600-ton luxury yacht I am enjoying my revenge as never before.

The Greek press, known for its accuracy and truthfulness, has picked up an item which appeared in an English newspaper concerning the *Spectator*'s 150th anniversary party. My name was briefly mentioned in it. How can a magazine use the byline of a known criminal, a tax dodger, asks Helen Vlacho's paper. Another one, with an even smaller circulation (hard to believe but true) demands that the authorities do something about discovering my whereabouts.

It all began with a libel case. Having written that the majority of the Greek press was not only yellow but on the take as well, I was sued, tried and convicted *in absentia*, eventually vindicated by a higher court that ruled what I had written was not libelous. In other words that parts of the Greek press *were* yellow and on the take.

Needless to say, the higher court's decision was never published by the Greek newspapers. For them I was, and shall remain, a fugitive from justice. And for good measure they have branded me a tax fugitive. But the purple prose of a yellow press is not my immediate problem. The twenty-five million people who have been huddling like refugees on the packed fringes of the Mediterranean are.

My cruise was supposedly to be a leisurely one. A slow sail down the French coast, through Italy on to Greece. But one look at the destruction of what was once an exceptionally beautiful coastline convinced my host to steam non-stop through the seemingly endless sprawling suburbia until we reached Corfu where I stepped ashore for the first time.

Here things were different. The myrtle and sage-smothered cliffs, the olive trees and statuesque cypresses, the arcaded cafés are all intact. Old, Italianate houses are in the majority. Unfortunately, so are Italian tourists. Bearded, smelly, wearing cheap sandals and socks inside their brief bikinis, the men swagger about talking about football. Their women, hairy-legged and fat-arsed, stagger around on stiletto heels looking for bargains. After the Italians come the Germans. They are almost as bad, if not as smelly. I ask a Greek how he can put up with it: 'I am only here to refuel my yacht,' he tells me. 'So are we,' I retort.

The *Anemos*, which means sea-breeze in Greek, was built in Holland twelve years ago. She is 70-feet long, has a 5000-mile range, cruises silently at fourteen knots and has a fresh water tank capacity of 50 tons enabling the ladies aboard to shampoo trice daily for a month.

Unlike most luxury yachts her exterior is tough looking and she is extremely sea worthy. The opulence begins when on board. Everything is teak, shiny stainless steel and glittering bronze. There are two cooks, a Frenchman and a Greek. Also three butlers, two maids and eleven crew.

Accommodation consists of five double cabins, each with bath, shower and bidet, plus the owner's suite which includes two bathrooms, a study, and a large bedroom.

The interior was designed by Jon Bannenberg, the Australian-born expert on gracious living afloat. My host is a music buff. Classical of course. The day begins with Mozart; there is Chopin before lunch, Beethoven before dinner, usually followed by Mahler. The evening always ends with Wagner. In Ithaka, among the bold and barren mountains which jut out of a coast indented by harbours and creeks, Brunnhilde's immolation scene becomes too much. We sing and throw glasses overboard.

TYRESOME

Porto Heli

Unlike Lord Byron who did not live long enough to take part in it, there is nothing that Greeks like more than an exodus. Perhaps it's the heroics of Missolonghi, or simply a self-destructive streak, that literally drives every Greek back to his or her village at the earliest opportunity, despite the fact that the chances of a safe return are slim. And as all Greeks come originally from poor villages, despite the airs they put on once in the big city, one can imagine the carnage that occurs whenever a big holiday weekend like Easter comes around.

Greeks are the most aggressive drivers in the world. At the wheel they like to gesticulate, beat their wives and children, examine the interiors of other passing cars and — needless to say — try to kill anyone who has the temerity or bad judgment to attempt to pass them. Because the roads are usually clogged with bodies during holidays.

I wisely bought myself a 72-foot yawl ten years ago, and thus have managed to survive. This year, however, I was faced with a small problem.

My boat, *Bushido*, used to have a crew of three. Although no one will believe this they were actually called Karamanlis, Papadopoulos and Grivas. I did not choose them for their names but for their great seamanship — together we had sailed from Sweden to Piraeus — but I must admit their names came in handy when people suggested I was not objective where politics were concerned. Well, last year, a midget-like shipowner named George Coumantaros, with a very long reach for such a short man, pinched all three of them from me by paying them enough money to ensure that they could become shipowners themselves within two years. They now work on his yacht and I have to make do with one new captain and a demented sailor.

Despite such hardships, I was determined to spend Easter in the islands with some British friends. There were a couple of Frasers, a Wellesley, and some others not chic enough to mention. The trouble began the day before they arrived, on Good Friday. My Mercedes coupé lived up to its name by being cut in half by a runaway truck. The driver was apparently absent-minded, or perhaps simply jealous, because he left the brake off his two-tonner when he stopped for a quick drink of retsina on a hill bordering my house.

Fortunately, I was not in the car when the accident happened. It was also fortunate for the driver that the police arrived in time to prevent me from turning him into yet another holiday casualty after he insisted that it was my parked Mercedes that had been at fault. (Greeks tend to accuse Mercedes owner of being despots, until, of course, they own one too.) Thus, when I met my British friends, driving a disgustingly cheap Datsun, their faces dropped in surprise and sympathy at my sudden economic demise. They dropped in even further, however, when they boarded my boat.

There was a force ten gale blowing and *Bushido* was pitching, rolling and heaving to an extent that would have made Admiral Nelson ill. After a while I took pity on them and told my captain to turn back. Then I ordered him to sail to Spetsai

and decided to drive the demoralised nobs to Porto Heli where
the boat would pick us up.

It was when we drove down the Pelponnese along a single
lane road that the Greek government euphemistically calls
Highway Number One that the real fun began. After three
dogs and two people had expired before our very eyes, a
certain ex-fiancée of Prince Charles began screaming and
begging me to turn back. So I got off the super olive-lined
and drove slowly through endless olive-lined dirt paths to
Epidaurus, hoping that the ancient Greek tradition would
prove more congenial to English sensibilities than the modern
one.

RICH, NOT RARE

Oddly enough Sigmund Freud was among the more recent
soi-disant wise men to have made the following ridiculous
claim: happiness, the Viennese genius said, is the adult
fulfilment of a childhood dream; children do not dream of
money; *ergo* money does not buy happiness.

As usual, Freud was wrong. The truly rich never pay for
anything, as somebody else is always happy to do that chore.
And as everyone knows the super rich never carry money with
them. I once witnessed a scene I thought impossible. I saw
the most parsimonious man I know, a certain Tommy Ford
from Detroit (no connection with the better Fords), actually
pick up the tab for Henry Ford II in the bar of the Hotel de
Paris in Monte Carlo. The barman did not know Mr Ford II.
And the deuce did not have money on him. Tommy Ford, who
has been known to walk up mountains when skiing rather
than pay for the ski lift, was only too happy to oblige.

Nor are the truly rich ever lonely, even when widowed. In
the case of truly rich women, losing a husband usually means
picking up a European title. There are thousands of noble
prospective bridegrooms waiting in the wings. When a truly
rich man is widowed — well, the perfect example is the case
of William Paley — the infighting among the ladies over his
soon-to-be octagenarian body manages to debase romantic
love to the level of some of his CBS programmes.

The truly rich never look behind them when they open a door and drop their coat. There is always somebody there to catch it. Equally, they never look behind them when they sit down at the dinner table. There is always a flunkey to push a chair beneath the gilded buttocks. If the merely rich were to attempt passing as truly rich by not looking behind them they would wind up with compression of the coccyx.

The truly rich do not have to chew. As Gloria Guinness once remarked, all one should eat is paté, caviar, soufflé and chocolate mousse. (But don't worry about their jaws shrivelling from under-development. Backbiting is good practice and nobody does it better than the truly rich.) They always carry two ounces of cocaine; peasants carry two grams. One famous Italian producer enjoys pointing to his nose in impressionable female company. 'One million dollars,' he says pointing at one nostril. Then he points at the other. 'One million dollars,' he repeats complacently.

The behaviour of the truly rich has no parallels with that of the merely rich. An aged, but accurate story, has the late Duke of Marlborough descending the stairway of a country-house one morning, waving his toothbrush in the air, and complaining that 'The damn thing doesn't foam.' It happened that the Duke's manservant had recently died and the new one was unaware of the fact that toothpaste had to be smeared on the brush before his grace used it.

The merely rich buy art: the truly rich buy artists. The truly rich are not bothered by things like guilt or introspection. Their insouciance borders on inhumanity. There is a perhaps apocryphal but indicative story of this insouciance. During a pheasant shoot at a truly rich estate during the heyday of the Austro-Hungarian empire, the host was informed by a servant that one of the guests had shot a pheasant on the ground. 'What?', roared the host with indignation at this unheard-of behaviour. 'Yes, sir' repeated the servant, 'The gentleman shot a peasant.' 'Oh, is that all, a peasant,' answered a relieved host, and the shoot went on.

Of course there is a catch to the unending happiness of the truly rich. As Logan Pearsall Smith pointed out, they have to live with the other rich and their families. And that is the true unhappiness that money can buy.

HILLBILLIES

Beverly Hills

In case anyone is wondering where all the rich Iranians have gone now that the Ayatollah has returned and is about to cut off the arms of those whose hands have been in the till, let me put their mind at rest. The very, very rich are here, among other rich exiles, and this small town of five square miles and 33,000 inhabitants is beginning to resemble a modern-day Noah's Ark for people worth more than a hundred million dollars.

Despite its size Beverly Hills does not suffer from an inferiority complex (although it seems that some of the denizens do, as there are more psychiatrists per head of population than anywhere on the planet). On the contrary, the town boasts the most outrageous, extravagant and super-fluous spenders in the world. Rodeo Drive, a two-and-a-half block strip of southern California's choicest real estate, is the focal point of the conspicuous consumption practised there. It makes New Bond Street, Rue Faubourg St-Honoré and Fifth Avenue look like Phnom Penh side streets after the Pol Pot takeover by comparison. It is a dazzling shopping area for sheikhs, stars and *nouveaus*, with one square inch of real estate estimated at more than £1.

Bijan Pakzad, an Iranian who got out while the getting was still good, spent £1 million on decoration alone for his exclusive men's store (he sells items like a £15,000 black cashmere topcoat lined with chinchilla). By trade estimates, Rodeo's 70-odd stores gross £300 million per annum. And the rush has just begun. The Gucci-Pucci kind of store that caters only to the very rich is just starting to come west. And no wonder, since the cheapest item on the whole drive is a £100 silk shirt.

Look, the American weekly magazine that closed down in 1971, has just been revived as a glossy fortnightly, and its main feature in the current issue is an eight-page spread on Beverly Hills buying. One multi-millionaire, an American, recently spent £50,000 splashing his wife's picture on bill-boards all over town (she wants to be an actress). Real estate values have soared by more than 300 per cent and £1 million

will not buy a house considered 'decent' — that is, it will be
with an outdoor-indoor swimming pool, a flood-lit tennis
court, or a servants' wing. Beverly Hills is redolent with
'anatomy asylums', as exercise parlours are euphemistically
called here, and despite the caviar and champagne excesses
there are no fat people anywhere in sight. There is also a very
brisk and expensive trade in face-lifts, hair-transplants,
wrinkle-removals and nose-jobs.

The only people besides the rich here are servants, police,
and private security guards. They make up the bulk of the
population. The only blacks are multi-millionaire rock stars
and the only industry is show business.

Given the above facts it is hardly surprising that expensive
trinket dealers are falling over themselves to establish a foot-
hold in the area. Teachers of Arabic are in such demand, in
fact, that some unscrupulous souls have taken unfair advantage. A recent example was the enterprising young stock-
broker who gave up his business in order to teach for higher
profits. The trouble was that he only spoke Yiddish and that
is the language he taught two Italian merchants. By the time
they found out he was long gone.

Recently the people of Beverly Hills were treated to a rare
sight: they saw sullen, unkempt, bullying men swaggering
around deserted factories and hospitals. Also rats and ten
foot-high uncollected rubbish heaps. Some of them thought it
was a science fiction film about the aftermath of a nuclear
holocaust and the ensuing civil chaos. But it wasn't a film. Just
satellite television pictures of London today. The outcome was
predictable: in order to get over their momentary depression
the money-mad locals ran out and did some more compulsive
buying.

TEMPS PERDU

Paris

Scott Fitzgerald was the undisputed master at evoking the loss
of youth, at portraying lives wrecked by over-indulgence and
irresponsibility. His heroes, nevertheless, like himself, never
lost their innocence, and that's what made them sadder in a

way. By comparison, Thomas Wolfe was more cynical and a lot more mature. Wolfe wrote that you can't go home again, that the boy, grown to manhood, can never return to the innocence of his childhood.

In Fitzgerald's 1931 short story, 'Babylon Revisited', Charlie Wales, the main character, returns to Paris after an absence of almost two years to find that things and people are not the way he left them. The stock market crash has wiped the glitter off the smart crowd, and the excesses of the Twenties have ravaged his old gang beyond recognition.

I thought of Fitzgerald last week in Paris. (And afterwards of Wolfe.) More to the point, the words of Charlie Wales came to mind as I drove to the Left Bank to see my daughter. 'I spoiled this city for myself. I didn't realise it, but the days came along one after another, and then two years were gone, and everything was gone, and I was gone.' Except that in my case it wasn't two years; it was more like ten. I hadn't lost my money or my health. No, among the desolation of the late Fifties and early Sixties, it was youth that I had left behind: among the Rubirosas, the Portagos, the various polo players, and places like the Elephant Blanc and Castel's.

Unfortunately for me, but fortunately in general, Paris never changes. The smells are the same, the taxi-drivers are the same, the Parisians are the same, as horrible as ever. Nostalgia is the city's cheapest commodity and everyone foreign gets it free. But it's not necessarily a good thing. Paris is a city to go to when in love. Not when suffering the pangs of unrequited adoration.

The barman of the Plaza-Athénée is an old friend. Like all barmen the world over he only talks about the good old days, when the clientèle was more elegant and people had more fun. So the barman and I talked about the past. Evoking memories of washed-up men and long-forgotten women, of empty bottles and smoky, half-filled rooms in the small hours of the night; of careless affairs and careless friendships and of many wasted hours, months, years.

It all seemed a blur last week as I left the Plaza for yet another party. It was a ball given by Nelson Seabra. He is a Brazilian, a member of the Grimaldi family, probably the nicest man who has ever owned a million pounds or has lived a life of total leisure. He's been a friend for 25 years and was best man at my wedding to the prettiest as well as silliest deb of a Paris season long ago. This year he decided to celebrate his 60th birthday with a ball in the grand manner. It was at the Pré Catalan, in the Bois, and 40 violin-playing hussars greeted the guests with pre-war czardas.

I was seated next to a lady whom I knew when she was too young to be allowed out. So I used to send her notes, and she would come to the polo and we'd look at each other across a field 300 feet wide. Nelson was seated between Princess Grace of Tax Exemption and Madame Barre, the Premier's wife. During a cabaret I strolled outside with my friend Mark Schand and Mick Jagger. We talked about the past, which to Mark is 1978. I went back in and saw more ghosts, people like Patino and Loel Guinness, always running away from taxes, always chic. I was the last to leave, saying an emotional goodbye to Nelson and to the ghosts coming out of the walls. Then I walked the streets again as dawn came up and had more sad memories. Had I really spent all that time doing the sort of thing I'd done tonight?

That's when I thought of Wolfe and even Hemingway. The latter wrote about Paris: 'She is a mistress, a fine place to be when quite young and it is a necessary part of a man's education. We all loved it once and we lie if we say we didn't. But she has other lovers now, so when we didn't love her any more we held it against her. But that was wrong because she is always the same age and she always has new lovers.'

CHARACTER REFERENCES

There seems to be an acute shortage of genuine eccentrics about at the moment and it's one that saddens me considerably. I don't expect everyone to behave like Squire Mytton — hardly anyone could afford to anyhow — but it would be refreshing if the social scene was graced and littered by a few more people who weren't heaven bent on being so utterly ordinary. Such is the shortage of oddities that a man has only to miss a train these days and he is immediately talked of as being bizarre.

Last week a publican, one of those dreadful men who think of themselves as being your 'genial host', leaned over his empty sandwich counter and said to me: 'You see that chap going out? He's a bit of a character.' I yawned to discourage him and said: 'Well, I mustn't keep you from your work', but he went on. 'Yes,' he said. 'Do you know that man must lose at least six umbrellas a year.'

Well, well. As I say, the shortage of eccentrics is acute, but you'd have thought that a man who meets as many people as a publican does could come up with something slightly more interesting than an umbrella loser. Casting a mind around my small circle of friends and acquaintances even I can produce a man who's in love with a coffee grinder at Fortnum & Mason, an antique dealer who was once voted 'Rat of the Week' by the old *Sunday Pictorial*, a doctor who's had a cold for five years and an ex-embassy press attaché who now writes the flagellation column for a seedy magazine with the help of his son's 50-year-old Burmese au pair girl.

But to draw attention to a mislayer of brollies, a mere forgetter of umbrellas, a man who'll go to all the trouble of subconsciously devising ways and means of going back to a pub, is appalling and rock bottom.

It makes me long for the days of Dennis Shaw, and to long for them a man has to be desperate for light entertainment. Shaw was an actor whose awful face was once known to thousands of film goers and whose activities were once known to all those on night duty at Savile Row police station. He weighed roughly 20 stone, was encrusted with warts and he drew attention to his very awfulness with unintentional moments of charm, sobriety and propriety.

He was usually cast as a villain, more often than not as a night club proprietor in English 'B' pictures, sometimes as a Gestapo man. Neither role taxed his talents to the full but unemployment and a shortage of readies brought out the best in him. His legend started just after the war and was summed up by the episode with John Le Mesurier. Shaw had been playing a lot of crooks in various films and the public had become used to seeing him nicked in the end. Le Mesurier came across him one night near Piccadilly when Shaw was drunk and being bundled into a Black Maria. Le Mesurier simply looked at him and said: 'Hallo, Dennis. Working?'

One of the things I liked most about Shaw was the way he always said and did what would only cross the minds of others. On one typical occasion in a night club — I think it was the Stork — Shaw, without a penny in his pocket, went right through the card. A meal with champagne, drinks for everyone and the obligatory bottle of Gordon's gin for himself. When he was presented with the bill he told them he hadn't any money. The head waiter shook his head and said: 'You remember what happened the last time you did this, Mr Shaw?' 'No. What happened?' asked Shaw. 'We sent for the police, sir,' said the waiter. 'Then send for the bastards again,' roared Shaw.

In spite of his behaviour he was an extremely difficult man to arrest and in spite of my great fondness for him our last meeting consisted of my attempting in vain to make a citizen's arrest. He caught me in a restaurant in Soho one night and there was no escape. He waited for me until I left and then he got into my taxi and refused to get out of it. I told the driver to go to Tottenham Court Road police station, which he did, and when we got there Shaw jumped out of the taxi and ran into the station. Moments later he appeared with four policemen, opened the taxi door and boomed out: 'Gentlemen. I'd like you to meet Jeffrey Bernard the biggest idiot in Soho.' He then sat down on the pavement. A policeman then put his head into the taxi window and said: 'We'd rather not arrest Mr Shaw, sir, if you don't mind. He's a bit difficult in the cells, you know.' The upshot was that they wouldn't have him at any price and Shaw knew it.

Shaw was also extremely fond of the telephone as a device for torture and when he phoned you long distance you couldn't help wondering which poor fool's telephone he was using. His calls also lacked finesse. Once, when John Le Mesurier lay in a distant hospital at death's door, Shaw got through to him and said: 'Hallo old man. I hear you're dying.' A bewildered and startled Le Mesurier replied: 'Oh dear. Am I?' 'Yes, old man. But I wonder if you could send me a couple of quid immediately.'

He may sound awful but he was really no more than particularly outrageous. We were in a television play together and rehearsing in a drill hall in Wandsworth when he turned up one morning with a carrier bag stuffed with dirty clothes. He handed the bag to the ingénue — it was her first job — and said: 'I'd like them back tomorrow morning, my dear. Hand-washed if you please, machines are so brutal.'

Only once did he really upset anyone to my knowledge and that was when a young actor quite rightly refused to buy two rounds on the trot. 'If you don't get another drink,' said Shaw, 'I shall jump up and down on the bonnet of your lovely new car.' The young actor held out and Shaw went through with his threats. The enormous Den Den, as he was known, with his jowls wobbling and stomach heaving like some hysterical and angry elephant, jumping up and down on the slowly sinking bonnet of a new car. I know the actor concerned and blame him for not standing up to Shaw, who in spite of his 20 stone loathed any form of violence.

What, I wonder, would the umbrella-loser have done had

he come face to face with Dennis Shaw in all his magnificent monstrousness? What indeed would the publican who pointed out to me the umbrella-loser have done with Dennis Shaw? He wouldn't have described him as being a 'bit of a character' anyway. No, Shaw was a man to be savoured. He was a collector's idem and he is sadly missed by many friends, head waiters and policemen. Come to think of it, he wouldn't have ever carried an umbrella. He would have taken someone else's.

LIFE OF RILEY

God dangled two carrots in front of me last week and I've decided to renew the onward plod. First, there was the new world record of alcohol found in human blood. Mr Sam Riley, 56, of Sefton Park, laid down his life in the creation of the record and, at the same time, broke the 1,000 milligram per 100 millilitres-of-blood barrier. Between Dionysus and Robert Newton there must have been thousands of attempts on the record, particularly, I imagine, by Russians and Scandinavians, but I'm tremendously proud that it should have been an Englishman who cracked it.

There's only one sour note that jangles a bit and that was the remark made by the coroner, Mr Roy Barter, at Riley's inquest. He recorded a verdict of 'accidental death' and the use of the word accidental smacks of sour grapes to me. Only once have I been into a pub accidentally and that was to The Mitre just off Hatton Garden where I went to get a watch strap mistaking it for a jeweller's. Riley's brother, George, giving evidence at the inquest added that the record-holder was a known alcoholic who lived alone and who drank as much as two bottles of whisky a day. That's another odd choice of word. You'd be hard pushed not to be 'known' if you drank two bottles a day and God knows how you'd do that accidentally. I'd be very surprised if Mr Riley thought he was drinking something else, although I did once meet a Turk in Islington who drank a bottle of whisky with every meal mistakenly thinking it was what he called 'English wine'.

No, we must give credit where credit's due — I imagine

Mr Riley must have had quite a lot of credit — and I hope you will join me in raising your next glass to a man who has finally heard the call for last orders.

The other bit of news that decided me not to give up the struggle was that of the industrial tribunal investigating the goings on at a jeweller's shop in Mansfield. A boy shop assistant was partly stripped by a counter girl who then bit him all over his back, and horseplay involved shopgirls and the manager rolling on the floor with their clothes disarranged. Best of all were the episodes involving what was called 'the crutch lift'. A Miss Stockdale developed this lift by putting her hands between Mr Bowskill's legs and lifting him up. They used to do this to each other every day and all I can say is that it all sounds a lot more interesting than the goings on at the offices of the *Spectator* or any other place of business I attend.

One hears so much depressing talk of this country's trouble nowadays and most of the blame is placed firmly at the feet of management and one can see why. There is a complete lack of communication. No liaison. Why weren't Mr Riley and Mr Bowskill brought together? Riley was an alcoholic living alone who probably needed a job and, by the sound of things, would have fitted in very nicely at the shop in Mansfield. As it is, they never met. Had they done so I imagine all kinds of assaults might have been made on a variety of world records. At the moment, I'm not quite sure what the record for a crutch lift under the influence of alcohol stands at but it would, presumably, have to be worked out on a complicated ratio involving weight lifted per 100 milligrams of alcohol per 100 millilitres-of-blood. This could have been text-book stuff and a very jolly way of teaching schoolboys chemistry and mechanics at the same time.

Obviously what's needed in this country is some sort of industrial personnel watch dog who'd see to it that the likes of Mr Riley should be employed in places like the Mansfield jeweller's shop. Failing that, those of us with similar bents should identify to each other by wearing T-shirts inscribed with phrases such as 'I AM A VERY SILLY PERSON'. We must stick together.

ONE LEG OVER

The past few days haven't been a lot of fun and the fact that
three quarters of the human race, including the entire media
force, were actually interested — to the point of obsession —
in some metal junk falling out of the sky, is probably indicative
of our being on the edge of another Dark Age. It seems to me
that we've been going through another of those phases in
which rock bottom is touched by nearly everyone. Idiots
abound.

One night recently, I climbed miserably into bed and had a
dream designed by Brueghel. In the morning, there wasn't a
single letter from a London publisher begging for my
presence. I examined the honeysuckle to see whether or not
it would bear the weight of my hanged body and then a passing
herdsman showed me something in the *Daily Mirror* which
was to lift me from the dark cavern of my depression to Olym-
pian heights of jibbering delight.

You may remember a similar black patch when we were
saved by Mr Sam Riley who laid down his life in breaking the
world record for alcohol consumption; now, that herdsman
brought me news of another great Englishman who had
emerged on the scene illuminating our darkest hour like a
Churchill. Our new, but unnamed, warrior and hero appeared
in Bodmin Crown Court last Monday week. He stood, all
5'6" of him in his stockinged foot — it wasn't reported
whether he wore a sock on the end of his artificial leg —
accused of raping a 17 stone, 16-year-old virgin in the front
seat of a van parked outside an abattoir.

It was alleged that the accused (known hereinafter as
'our hero') forced the ample Cornish lady across the gearbox,
handbrake and seat-belt clips, held her down with one hand
and removed her knickers with the other. This makes Drake's
effort at *sang froid* with his game of bowls seem almost
hysterical to me.

Counsel for the defence, out-Rumpoling Rumpole, got
straight to the crutch of the matter when he inquired of the
hitherto unsullied girl, 'If you are telling the truth, he
managed to lift 17 stone with one hand'. The victim said, 'I

saw his false leg after he got his trousers down. It was from the knee-cap down'. All good stuff, but the cherry on top of the icing came when our hero admitted to the police that he had sex with the girl and claimed that she consented. 'But,' he added, 'I didn't enjoy it.' The following day he was found not guilty.

Now there happen to be several interesting aspects of this case as I pointed out to my dear wife in my summing up. 'In the first place,' I told her, 'you must, as has become the practice these days, regard the victim as a hostile witness, hell-bent on producing a Greek tragedy and you must therefore disregard most of her evidence. She allowed a man, an almost defenceless amputee, who was in a drunken state, to drive her down a dark lane to an abattoir, from where, she stated, she was too frightened to run away. Too frightened to run away from a one-legged man! I ask you!

'Wouldn't you say,' I continued addressing my still sceptical wife, 'that it was more likely that the accused was the victim of what is known among the lower orders as having been given a "sympathy-leg-over"? Is it not a well-known fact that a sentimental and crusading streak in women obliges them to give their bodies willy-nilly to amputees, unpublished poets, potential suicides and all manner of little boys lost and would you deny that his cavalier statement to the police to the effect that he had not enjoyed said congress to be a wounding remark and one that would make her entire 17 stone quiver with indignation?

'Finally, would you not agree that the accused stands not only nearly legless by surgical definition but nearly legless in so far as he was unable to remember the night of the alleged rhapsody beyond the fact that he didn't enjoy it? I put it to you, you can only bring in one verdict. Take your time.'

'Not guilty,' said my wife, 'but I bet he *did* enjoy it, whatever it was.'

I sat there, another case closed, feeling sure that our other hero, Mr Sam Riley, was turning in his grave with delight.

TO MURIEL

I suppose the final joke was that Muriel Belcher should have died on Hallowe'en and then been buried on Guy Fawkes Day She certainly would have appreciated it and members of the Colony Room Club can well imagine how she would have laughed sitting on her stool at the end of the bar like a raven on its perch. Well, she has fallen off her perch and the news came through to Soho just minutes after a memorial service was held at St Paul's, Covent Garden, for the actor Sean Lynch who died in Spain just a few days before. A depressing week indeed for all those who have been using the Colony Room since it opened in 1948 and who also either worked with Sean or knew him from Gerry's Club.

I'm afraid I have to be very personal about Muriel since I know very few facts about her except that she originally came from Birmingham to London, worked for a time in Harrods, and eventually took over a Club near the Haymarket before establishing her unique watering hole in Dean Street. I was rather intimidated by her when I first met her — she *always* commanded a sort of respect — and, in those days, the club was actually quite posh. She never minced words about the fact that she really only wanted rich, famous, successful titled people as members, but she made an exception with a few of us provided those same rich, famous . . . people spent plenty of money on us layabouts. Neither did Muriel mince her language which was as strong as her wit was quick.

There was the bald-headed man well known for his compulsive verbosity. He walked in one afternoon and said, 'Muriel, I'm worried, I've got to go to a fancy dress party tonight and I can't think what to go as.' She fixed him with a smile and said, 'Why don't you go as a bald-headed cunt?' Language apart, there was something almost outrageous about her 'campness'. Sometimes she seemed convinced the world was populated entirely by homosexuals — she called most men as well as women either Kate or Mary — and her attitude towards Len Blackett illustrates a little her 'knowingness'. Blackett — long since dead himself — was a charming old queen who worked in the city and drank scotch for England

in the Colony in the evening. He was, more or less, a hostess
and it so happens that he'd won the Military Cross in 1916
when he was a Captain. Anyway, whenever anyone asked
Muriel about Blackett she'd say: 'She was a very brave little
woman at the Somme.' Apart from that sort of remark I can
still hear the general patter quite clearly. 'Come on cunty,
spend up. You're not buying enough champagne. Are you a
member sir? No? Come on then, fuck off. Members only.' She
won't just be missed, she has been missed ever since the
beginning of her long illness, and all those of us who knew her
will continue to raise our glasses — far too frequently — to
drink to her. And that's just what she would have liked.

FRANK NORMAN

I'd like to make a particularly personal tribute to Frank
Norman who died on 23 December bringing 1980 to such a very
sad end for so many of us. I don't want to harp on about the
history of his career — that's been done — and we know he
wrote 16 books that included *Bang to Rights* and *Banana
Boy* plus four plays including *Fings Ain't What They Used
to Be*. I just want to recollect and savour some of the happenings that involved us both during the 30 years I knew him and
which spanned the hooligan days of the early Fifties through
to the wild and successful days of the Sixties and then to the
recent tongue-in-cheek mellowness which spread benignly
during the Seventies. I say 'mellow' although I know you can
stir up an old wasp's nest, but Frank, until very recently,
looked to be cruising through middle age, happy with his
wife Geraldine, one novel a year and a Friday-only visit to
Soho to give a master class. That Soho is dying we know, but
that one of its more distinguished features should be so
suddenly and cruelly demonished makes me wonder what on
earth is God up to? I doubt that Heaven knows.

Memories of Frank merge and blur. When I first met him in
a café called the Alexandria in Rathbone Place — he was
later to use it and the layabouts in it for his play *A Kayf Up
West* — he caught my and everyone's attention with his

aggression or at least his aggressive looks which were high-
lighted by a razor scar. He was pretty distant in those days,
a little broody, and he made an amazing attempt to settle
down at one point when he got married and set up as a newsagent, of all things, in the village of Boxford in Suffolk. Can
you imagine it? Of course, he got as bored as hell with it. He'd
pop up to London in his car, get drunk in the Stork Club, drive
back to Boxford at four in the morning and, of course, the
papers would get delivered at lunchtime. Well, that didn't
last long.

What else springs to mind? The Ad Lib Club. That was in
the days when it had just become fashionable to import
piranha fish and keep them as pets. The tank in the Ad Lib
represented a challenge to Frank, so he took off his jacket,
rolled up his shirt sleeve and plunged his arm into the tank.
They didn't even give him a nibble, which disappointed him
deeply, but he then mounted the stage and sang 'Falling in
Love with Love is Falling for Make Believe'.

There was the epic fight in Gerrard Street. He somewhat
foolishly wrote a piece in the *Evening Standard* which said
that the man he'd shared a cell with when he was in the nick
was a grass. Eventually the grass was sprung and came looking for Frank. My brother and I were unfortunate enough
to be with Frank when the grass and 14 of his companions
caught up with him. Frank ended up in hospital, but he
showed tremendous guts in a fight reminiscent of Brando's
effort in *On the Waterfront*.

Our efforts to collaborate on the book we did together,
Soho Night and Day (he wrote it and I took the pictures), were
something of a farce. We'd wander around Soho all day and
night having hospitality heaped on us by publicans and
restaurateurs who wanted to appear in the book and I suppose
we were drunk for a year. When we weren't given hospitality,
Frank paid for everything.

That generosity sums him up for me. We had some fearful
rows but his sort of generosity would end them. He had
tremendous loyalty towards his friends and was so much a
warmer person than the 'scar-faced ex-jailbird' he called
himself. *The Times* cut a sentence I wrote about him — not

the sort of thing *The Times* would like. I said that he negated
that ghastly cliché 'You only get out of life what you put into
it'. Frank put an awful lot into it, and I wish he'd got a little
more out of it than he did. We all knew him far too briefly.

ANTICIPATORY

'May I add a few words to your excellent obituary of Jeffrey
Bernard. I knew him intimately for forty-six years and I feel
that many of his more remarkable qualities were left unsung
in your otherwise comprehensive review of his messy life. He
was born in 1932 — probably by mistake — covered from
head to food in eczema. One of the first things he did was to
wet the bed and he continued to do so until he was fifteen.
A weak, thin-skinned and over-sensitive boy, he had few
friends at school. He usually chose to sit at the very back of
every classroom so that he could play with himself unobserved
and the only subject at which he excelled was history. His
liking for historical biography was an early sign of the paranoia he was to develop later but his early obsession with sex
prevented him from obtaining any worthwhile academic
honours. By the time he left school he had become a chain
smoker and compulsive writer of fan letters to Veronica Lake.
'In 1946 he paid his first visit to Soho and from that point he
was never to look forward. It was here in the cafés and pubs of
Dean Street and Old Compton Street that he was to develop
his remarkable sloth, envy and self-pity. Well do I remember
his first bouts of drunkenness that usually ended in tears or
abortive suicide attempts and I think that it must have been
at this time that we began to realise that Bernard was not cut
out for a career as a naval officer as his mother had hoped.
'He drifted from job to job and between jobs he spent
months at a time accepting small sums of money from homosexuals or friends who were working. He began to develop a
greed for unearned money and the growing conviction that he
was cut out for better things. After a short, undistinguished
spell in the army from which he was given a medical discharge,
his pay book being marked "Mental Stability Nil", he returned

to Soho, got married and split up with his wife a few weeks later.

'It was during this period that he first became involved with horse-racing and gambling and the feelings of infantile omnipotence that this prompted were to last him the rest of his life. These feelings were particularly noticeable in his dealings with women and some even said that his life was a never ending cliché of a search for his mother. His drinking began to escalate to such an extent that he was unable to hold down the most ordinary of jobs and he was consequently advised to take up journalism. Even in this field it was noticeable that he was never offered a staff job and he gradually drifted into writing a series of personal and, at times, embarrassing columns and articles about his own wretched experiences.

'After a spell in the alcohol and drug addiction unit at St Bernard's Hospital, Hanwell, he developed the fantasy that starting tomorrow it would all be different. Under the growing conviction that geographical changes would solve his problems he moved to the country and lived in various 'dream' cottages. Unfortunately, he was always there too. My last memory of Bernard was of seeing him staring at his typewriter one weekend and fighting yet another battle against his chronic amnesia. He leaves two unwritten books and a circle of detached acquaintances.'

7. ENDANGERED SPECIES: *Taki*

OFF THE GAME

According to one connoisseur, backgammon champion of Greece and man-about-Mayfair, John Zographos, the high class tart is one more victim of socialism and the drab, egalitarian society. Piero de Monzi, a shop-owner in London, sees the problem differently. Monzi is of the opinion that HCTs have disappeared because of fashion's uniformity and the upper class obsession in following a downmarket conformity.

Only one of the cognoscenti interviewed mentioned morality. This was Joe Dwek, European backgammon champion, born in Cairo of Lebanese parentage, owner of a British passport and a grand house in Chester Square. Joe, an articulate and extremely resourceful young man, voiced his anger and sadness over the vanishing HCTs. 'There was no greater bakshish than a high class tart. Our whole way of life in Egypt centred around ways of showing our appreciation for past favours by discovering new and beautiful women who were corrupt. Even when I came to England ten years ago, I still enjoyed the pleasures of an HCT with my friends. But now, moral standards have collapsed and everyone does it. All the girls are corrupt. Even Quasimodo could get a girl without paying today. It is horrible.'

Whatever the reason, it is an undeniable fact that London is badly in need of high class tarts. Leaving the aesthetics apart the economic principle alone would be enough to warrant a government inquiry. Because in the meantime thousands of

randy foreigners are taking their lucrative business elsewhere.

Often they would spot fun-girls willing to go on fun-trips on
their yachts, and then hand over a watch or bracelet as a
down-payment. Needless to say all this activity generated the
transfer of a lot of funds; but not any more.

The system is at fault. It favours quantity over quality, mass
production over uniqueness and facility over challenge. The
writing was on the wall already way back in 1963. Tarts like
the ones who brought down the Tory government then could
not — in the opinion of another expert — get arrested as they
say. They were second class. And it got progressively worse.
Another Tory minister got caught with a third class tart. And
like all third class tarts she sang.

The way things are now is an affront to a once honourable
and discerning profession. Tarts work through hall porters
in large hotels around Marble Arch and Hyde Park Corner.
They charge between £50 and £100 and cater mostly to Arabs.
Even taking into account these inflationary times, such sums
would once have procured bi-lingual, sophisticated models,
or even little known *ingenues* waiting for the big break. No
longer. One should consider oneself lucky to get even a
woman. Some customers have had unpleasant surprises.

The jet-set — which got its name when HCTs were paid to
fly around the globe by sugar daddies — has managed once
again to skirt this problem. Although HCTs were once its
only source of relaxation and entertainment, they are now all
but forgotten. This was perspicaciously managed by the
introduction of cocaine. He who sniffs is not randy. Also, he
who sniffs a lot thinks sex is a dirty word. Thus pushers make
the bread and mum remains hungry.

Given the above, one must conclude that inflation, socialist
principles, lack of morality, the welfare state and the British
character have all contributed to the ruin of high class tart-
dom. As one ex-madame told me: 'Girls today *try* and make
themselves ugly. They latch on to the first peasant they sleep
with. They drop out, have no ambition and no class. The
person who coined the phrase "I'm doing my own thing"
should be lynched.'

PARTY MEN

Although social climbing is as prevalent as ever in café society, the costume ball, the *pièce de resistance* of a successful climb, is becoming as rare as Italian war heroes or Puerto Rican aristocrats. Instead, getting wrecked and overstimulated in a profusion of sounds, strobe lights, disco music and pills in a psychedelic setting is the *in* thing of the Eighties.

Needless to say, social climbers are ecstatic over disco culture and its fascinating amalgam of nobs and punks, rich and poor, square and trendy. Like air travel prices, cut throat competition among the Beautiful People has reduced refinement to hip, eccentricity to conformity, and nuance to sensory overkill. And only a blue jean is needed to become an eligible climber.

Gone are the days when South American parvenus like Charlie Bestegui, a Mexican millionaire, would take over Venice, dress up three-quarters of her population and import all the right people on private trains. After making his mint, the Mexican wanted to make it in Europe and he went about it in style. He always attired himself in Louis XV costumes, and his pock-marked face helped lend credence to the disguise. Managing to combine unheard of things like taste, ingenuity and flamboyance, Bestegui also spent money as if it was going out of style. And he was successful. Admitted to the innermost sanctums of European aristocracy, he left an indelible mark that survived both him and his fortune. He fathered a daughter who today carries one of the oldest and grandest titles in Spain. He managed this by seducing the wife of a famous duke, his affair with her becoming common knowledge to everyone but the old gentleman.

Bestegui always said that if it wasn't for his flair for party giving he would have remained a peon in aristocratic eyes. But because of it by the end of his life people referred to him as a Spanish grandee.

Another great party-giver who used the costumed extravaganza as a vehicle to more gentle company and surroundings was the Marquis de Cuevas of ballet fame. Cuevas, a Chilean, who was no more a marquis than my colleague Jeffrey

Bernard, but unlike Jeffrey, who spends his time in Soho bars and likes to frequent yobs and rummies, Cuevas preferred upward mobility and European palaces.

In a classic case of one-upmanship, he outflanked Bestegui by arriving in Europe unknown but with a title. The first thing he did after acquiring his honorific from an impoverished Portuguese farmer was to start giving balls. His last shindig was almost twenty years ago but people still are talking about it. It took place in Biarritz and Cuevas came dressed as Louis XIV. (I hope readers will notice the one-upmanship.) He took over the Golf Club de Chiberta, transformed it into a seventeenth-century chateau and arrived last, on a throne carried by eight flunkies. Poor little rich girl Barbara Hutton entered riding on an elephant. The Duke of Brissac, France's premier duke, came as a Monmartre pimp. The party cost 50,000 pre-inflation pounds.

South Americans had cornered the social climbing market in post-war days. Antenor Patino, Bolivian tin heir of cocoanut tree into Rolls-Royce fame, cannot be ignored when balls and climbing are mentioned. The diminutive Patino has been giving parties for almost half a century and is the only climber alive today. Although still climbing he is attuned to the times and has not given a party in exactly ten years. His last took place in Estoril and probably had a lot to do with the subsequent Portuguese military uprising. It was rumoured that the coup leaders had served as waiters at the ball.

The party-giver who served as a bridge between the good old days of climbing and today's disco freaks was not a Latin, however. Alexis de Rede, né Rosenthal in Vienna, was the first party giver and ascendant *extraordinaire* to indulge in *nostalgie de la boue*. In other words, inviting creeps, punks, black leathered gays and trendies. The aristocracy loved it. Dukes, Princes and Earls mixed with black hair dressers, rock stars and dress designers. Rede made it but in the process of doing so put the ball business in moth balls. Drugs did the rest along with voyeur journalism. Why spend money, alert the taxman, give an opportunity to the gossip columns to have a field day only to be read by people one would not be caught speaking to even if marooned on a desert island, when

you can climb with anyone your heart desires simply by
hanging around a loo of a smokey disco and pretending to
sniff?

Resembling primitive tribal religious rites, today's orgies
differ from the grand parties of yesterday as snuff from
cocaine. Although similar in nature and purpose they are as
dissimilar as night and day. And there is no hope in sight.
One of the greatest social climbers around, an American
oil-man, plans to corner the market of Beautiful People and
hoi polloi by building a house with loos the size of drawing
rooms and vice versa.

HUSTLING

St Moritz

Now that luxury liners have gone the way of high button
shoes, honourable politicians and thin African guerrilla
leaders, card sharks and backgammon hustlers have been
forced to abandon their natural habitat and come in from the
wet. They are now crawling all over Gstaad, St Moritz, Palm
Beach and Acapulco during winter, and Monte Carlo, Cap
d'Antibes, Deauville and Marbella during summer. London,
Paris, New York and Los Angeles serve as main hunting
grounds the rest of the year.

And like everything else, everything traditional that is, the
hustlers themselves have changed. They used to be known for
their impeccable manners, faint Balkan or mid-Atlantic
accents, gomina groomed hair, sartorial splendour, athletic
prowess and dancing ability. But with the exception of two (an
Englishman and a Frenchman) hustlers today remind one of
Runyonesque characters without the warmth and certainly
without the humour.

They are a seedy crowd, nearly all male, sporting gold
chains, nylon shirts, platform shoes and small diamond
rings on their pinkies. No elegant lady with long cigarette
holder ever looks over their victim's shoulder and signals
his cards. Technology has taken care of that too. A slob friend
sitting thirty yards away and wearing high-powered sun-

glasses signals him electronically. Who needs women? Who needs elegance?

Needless to say, the hustlers are simply following tradition. The collapsed standards regarding dress, speech and manners have simply made it easier for anyone bent to hustle. They fade out among the crowds in grand resort hotels like tiger-suited guerrillas in the jungle. Once the rich pigeon has been spotted and lured to the table, it is impossible to tell the shark from the victim. Both look horrible.

The newest enthusiasm of the Bored and Beautiful (in reality the Cynical and Ugly) is the game of backgammon. It was once described as a game for the higher classes which had never been vulgarised or defiled by uneducated people. Nothing, however, could be further from the truth. Backgammon has become such a status symbol that no gay assistant hair-dresser in Los Angeles or black dope-peddler in Harlem would be caught dead without his Asprey's leather executive case.

Card sharks have been dealt a cruel blow when gin rummy and poker went out of style. (American hustlers always know how to manipulate dice, because of crap games.) Skills which took a lifetime to perfect, such as hitting seconds or dealing from the bottom of the deck, had to be abandoned. Now it is imperative to be able to control one dice by dipping a finger in the cup or be an electrical expert and wire the backgammon board or the table it's placed upon.

Many old timers could not keep up with the trend. Some were too old to learn the new tricks. Others simply refused to debase themselves and specialise in a game played by every fellah in Middle Eastern cafés for centuries. A new breed of hustler came into being.

Despite the new etiquette and crashing standards there is still some hope. The most successful hustlers are two gentle-men (mentioned previously) who have refused to join the great unwashed brigade of sharks, and with terrific results to show for it. Mind you they are hardly Beau Brummels but both refrain from growing the nail of their little finger in order to show they are not indulging in manual labour.

The French member of the *entente cordiale* has the dex-terity of a Houdini as well as being one of the best players in the world. His real talent, however, lies in his thespian ability. This giant of a man puts Lord Olivier to shame by managing to convince one and all that he is an easy mark. He specialises in pigeon killing; that is when his English partner comes in.

Once the 'apple' has been stripped by the Frenchman, the perfidious Englishman (a minor-public-school man) approaches him and proposes an alliance. Greed being a common human trait the victim usually agrees. And that is when the fun begins. Backgammon is a game which gives the impression that instinct is more important than a scientific approach. The Englishman being a player known throughout the world for his virtuosity in backgammon, it is a rare person who refuses to follow his advice. Needless to say the advice sometimes backfires as the wrong play turns out at times to be the right one. That is when strange encounters begin taking place. A trip to the loo costs the victim a fortune as the Englishman loses a 64 game. ('Where were you? We were winning a double game and then he threw four double sixes.') Mysterious calls, usually from girls, take the 'mark' out of the room with the same results.

This year alone the pair have made over a hundred thousand pounds. In public they abuse each other to such an extent that hostesses are embarrassed to invite them to the same party. Notwithstanding their recent winnings (last year was their best ever) they are now very depressed. The reason is the financial demise of an elderly Greek who could be relied upon when Italian, Spanish or German financiers had to go to the office. The elderly victim has been going blind slowly but continued to play the pair relying on their . . . honesty. After the shipping crash, however, it was curtains. All of a sudden the pair discovered his accent to be vulgar and his habit of swearing in Greek unacceptable.

CLAUDE'S REIGN

Paris

A politically motivated act has just abolished one of the most sacrosanct of Gallic institutions. In a gesture reminiscent of the

pre-election purification ritual perfected by Mayor Daley of
Chicago and Jimmy Walker of New York, the authorities have
not only done away with the institution, they have arrested
the high priestess as well. The shrine I am referring to,
needless to say, is the incomparable call-girl service of
Madame Claude, run so efficiently by her *Dauphine*, Mlle
Catherine Virgitie.

Madame Claude's main office, located above the stolid
Banque Rothschild, on the avenue George V, is occupied by
a squad of evil-looking gendarmes, and the best-known
number in the history of Alexander Graham Bell's invention
has been disconnected. The reasons for this brutal and icono-
clastic act are political. The communists who along with the
socialists are favourites to win the coming elections, have
attacked the regime for turning a blind eye to the greatest
French attraction since the Louvre. But for the benefit of any
reader who might not be familiar with Madame Claude here is
a brief resumé.

A tiny brunette with a strong personality and a pleasant
smile, Claude Grudet spent four years in a German concentration camp. She attributes her consummate hatred of the
communists to the cynical methods the Reds used to escape
their fate. She claims they denounced non-communists and
the well-to-do to the Germans after having become friendly
with the victims. After the war she married a resistance hero
and became the most successful Madame in history by apply-
ing the Geisha principle. Men were not fawned upon only to
be hurried and treated like cattle once the price was paid.

On the contrary, money was never mentioned, special
clients were allowed to open accounts, thus not cheapening the
experience by having to come up with the cash, and the girls
were not . . . 'professionals'. The young ladies were mostly
models, struggling actresses and dancers. Some were happily
married and supplemented their income. All were educated,
spoke foreign languages and bought their clothes in the
boutiques of the best couturiers. They acted as perfect
hostesses and were taught to do so by Claude. The quality
was such that two of France's most popular actresses today
began their careers with Claude. A beautiful and youthful

countess, a German by birth, also took her first steps in society through Claude. So did the wife of a great Arab entrepreneur.

The distinguishing feature of ex-Claude girls who have made good is their lack of pomposity as well as the friendliness they display towards ex-clients who have become their social inferiors. As most French society leaders began as demi-mondaines, the unassuming manner of Claude girls manages to disarm even the bitchiest of gossips. Claude reigned supreme during the 'sixties and early 'seventies. A call would provide the client with the description of available girls, her size, colour of hair, sexual preference, etc. There was never any exaggeration of the girl's beauty, Claude believing — unlike most of her rival *entremetteuses* — that a pleasant surprise is the greatest aphrodisiac.

The prices were high, twenty pounds for one hour, fifty pounds for the night. But when oil-rich Arabs came on the scene the end was in sight. Two thousand pounds was not an unusual price to pay for an afternoon's pleasure, and, needless to say, that eliminated most Europeans. Claude saw the writing on the wall, wrote her memoirs and turned over her business to Catherine Virgitie, her most beautiful and nicest girl. Catherine disliked Arabs and wanted to work on the business side.

When French political activists turned promiscuity into a mode of political protest, Claude and Catherine became the target of communist attacks. Claude counter-attacked, pointing out the Reds as frightening examples of sexual bankruptcy. She painted a nightmare world where sex was forbidden citing Orwell and *1984*. The inept and frightened Giscard, leaning over backwards to appease the Left, reluctantly gave the orders to close her down.

The institution of Madame Claude provided a great service to the Fifth Republic. Both De Gaulle and Pompidou used its offices for entertaining recalcitrant heads of state. Thus it was ironic that an ex-Prime Minister, Gaullist to the bone, explained the closure as the 'first insidious sign of British subversion the General had warned us against. No sooner have the British come into the Common Market than Madame Claude is shut down. Soon we will have to create men's clubs, develop a sense of humour and forget about women altogether. Merde.'

RUINED CITY

Athens

The birthplace of democracy is in decline from noise, pollution and heavy traffic. In fact, it is now acknowledged that Athens is an endangered city. After a six-month absence I was shocked to see further decline in the quality of life, something I thought impossible. Yet more horrible buildings have been built, more cars imported, more people have left the countryside in search of El Dorado in the big city.

That Athens has been allowed to deteriorate to such a degree is totally due to official acquiescence to greedy speculators. For once, however, not the kind usually associated with private enterprise. On the contrary. These greedy men are part of the state apparatus: an unholy alliance of government bureaucrats and civil engineers has managed to turn the once beautifully unique, neo-classical city into a nightmare of granite matchboxes, plastic and neon. It is the second most polluted city after Osaka.

It wasn't so long ago that being rich in Athens was considered better than being rich anywhere in the world. And the quality of life kept the poor from complaining. The climate made village life idyllic and the excesses of the rich were witnessed only by a few. Then politicians decided that the countryside was too closely tied to the church and the traditions of the past. Greece needed industry in order to better her lot. The countryside emptied as federal grants went only to city dwellers. This was after the second world war and the communist uprising which killed most village teachers and priests.

One third and more of all Greeks live in Athens and its suburbs — three and a half million of them. The government plays a larger role in their lives than in any other supposedly free country. All basic industries are state-owned. Banking, telecommunications, electricity, transport, railways, all natural resources and, indirectly through banking, even insurance companies. There are laws for every occasion, even one that tells the citizen when he can drive his car at weekends. (Odd and even numbers on the licence plates decide.)

The plight of Athens is only another manifestation of a political tradition that has sacrificed the interests of the majority — as well as the future welfare of the country — to immediate expedience and political gain. For the politicians, however, there is a redeeming feature in all this chaos and misery: the overcrowded neighbourhoods, the poorly-designed apartment houses, the screeching tyres, blaring horns, and tension-ridden hours spent struggling through the traffic that chokes the city, cause disenchantment. And demagoguery thrives on disenchantment and alienation.

Greek politicians have traditionally preached the womb-to-tomb kind of socialism; they have fought against the kind of education that teaches a craft. Thus thousands of university graduates of sociology are busy painting the city's walls red with anarchical slogans. Old-fashioned values, however, prevail, and Greeks still believe in their elders, their religion and the sanctity of the family. If it wasn't for such traditions the country would probably be in worse shape than Italy.

Athenians are political animals. Rumours and gossip thrive in every corner café. The press reflects the public's taste and is in turn recognised as the yellowest and most subjective in the world. The press has been free since the fall of the colonels and has concentrated its vitriol against the West in general and the Greek shipowners in particular. It is not too difficult to understand why. The West and the shipowners represent the kind of world Marxists do not like. They have altered the seamen's life and brought more wealth into Greece than even the Marshall Plan. The state, however, does not like it. If people are allowed to strike it rich and help their fellow citizens what will happen to bureaucrats?

8. THE BORING, THE UGLY AND THE DAMNED:
Taki and Jeffrey Bernard

UGLY WOMEN: A TREATISE: *Taki*

Remember the old joke about the Russian diplomat visiting New York and having a prostitute sent to his room courtesy of his contacts at Amnesty International? The Soviet biggie starts to undress her, but as soon as he has a glimpse of her calf he complains about the lack of hair. 'What, no wool?' he moans. He gets more annoyed when he realises that she even shaves her armpits. 'Why no wool? I like wool,' he keeps repeating. Finally, after his groaning has reached a fever pitch, the hooker has had enough. She turns toward the representative of the United Soviet Socialist Republic and tells him: 'Hey Bud, what do you want to do, knit or fuck?'

I used to think this joke was funny, and indicative of the ugliness of Russian women, whom I always considered among the ugliest, if not the ugliest in the world. As painful as this confession may be, however, I must admit that I was wrong. And if this weren't enough, guess who I have concluded are the ugliest? Yes, horror of horrors, the Americans. As incredible as it may sound, my opinion is based on scientific research, not emotions. But before anyone starts to throw stones, let me explain how I arrived at my findings.

It is an accepted fact that true beauty is a combination of body and spirit. Just as true is the fact that a woman lacking femininity cannot possibly be considered beautiful in the true and classical sense of the word. In fact I'll go further than that. A good figure and regular features detract from, rather than enhance, the appearance of a woman lacking femininity. How does one define femininity? Easy. A feminine woman possesses qualities which make her as different from a man psychologically as she is physically. That is, she is passive, cunning, patient, motherly, a homebody, monogamous, etc. Furthermore, a feminine woman defines herself almost exclusively by her relationship to man, and is sculpted accordingly. If this sounds far-fetched, it shouldn't. Four-hundred million years of field experiments have proved that the female is sculpted differently from the male for the above reasons.

Thus the human's closest species, the macaque, is bigger than his female counterpart, stronger, and the one who decides if and where they will move their breeding grounds. The male will respond to outside dangers, while the female remains unconcerned. She will continue feeding the young or grooming herself while the male stalks the enemy. She knows the male is responsible.

Does this sound familiar? Of course it does. That's how it was until a few ugly women who could not get men to like them decided to change something that is as unchangeable as, well, for lack of a better example, man and woman. John Aspinall, the English sage who breeds wild animals in his two private zoos in Kent, believes that a woman's trust consolidates the man's dominance. Without it, the male tends to lose his masculinity. One does not have to be a scientist or an anthropologist to see that this makes sense. Look what is happening now. Ever since women decided not to trust men, that men were almost expendable, there has been a marked increase in pederasty. The phenomenon has been widely observed.

Aspinall contends that every male has a 70 to 30 per cent hormone count. Seventy per cent male hormones, thirty per cent female. Every female is the opposite. (Again, before anyone starts to shout, these are rough estimates. Exact figures are for jargon-artists trying to mislead through statistics.) As the state has taken over the male (or father) role, the male species has come to feel disrobed, his position usurped. The only function left to him by the omnipotent state is to pay bills and attend to the occasional derelict relative. Even his old familiar role as warrior has been challenged.

Some women, although I doubt their hormone count is 70 to 30, now try to compete by being soldiers. America now has 44 per cent more female soldiers than all the world's other armies combined.

Which brings us to the subject of why some women are unique. Like Mrs Thatcher, whose male hormone count has risen dramatically ever since she found herself surrounded by males without enough male hormones. Looking at the state of Small Britain today I am not surprised. Mrs Thatcher, unlike Cleopatra or Elizabeth I or Catherine the Great, all of whom inherited their fathers' dynastic strength, entered a vacuum left by males suffering from a very low testosterone count. (Socialists, trade union leaders, intellectuals, are notoriously effete.)

Mull this over for a while, and I believe you will agree that despite outward appearances a woman can be truly ugly. Take Jane Fonda and Shirley MacLaine. That harshness, those granite glares, the shrillness of their rhetoric — it makes one want to shriek at their ugliness. This is less true when one is confronted with the ruins of remarkable ugliness, as in the case of Lillian Hellman. (See what I mean about good figures and regular features detracting from rather than enhancing one's appearance? Hellman's revolting features do not make her any uglier than her ugly rhetoric and pathetic lies. In Fonda's case and MacLaine's, they do.)

Maggie Scarf, the female science writer, has proved beyond any reasonable doubt that John Bowlby's 'attachment theory' is correct. Bowlby, an Englishman, says that a female needs to connect through emotional bonding. This she manages through a behavioural mechanism, a trait that has found its way into the female genetic code. Scarf points out that emotional bonding, once a key to survival for the weaker sex, now causes nothing but trouble as women are caught between the demands of their genes — to be feminine, obedient, married — and a society telling them that they are equal and independent. Feminists are not only making women become uglier, but unhappier as well. Feminism is a brutal hoax.

So, now that we have established once and for all that America's liberated women are the ugliest, precisely which of these ugliest is ugliest? But remember. It is not important who is ugliest, but what makes her ugly.

Not to include leading women libbers among the ugliest would be like leaving the corn out of Kansas. Gloria Steinem, Marge Piercy, Adrienne Rich, Phyllis Chesler, Susan Brownmiller, the aforementioned Fonda and Warren Beatty's sister, as well as some others too ugly for me to want to recall. Then there are Bella Abzug and Diane Von Furstenberg, that nice Jewish girl from Belgium who married her gay prince and made millions selling clothes under his name, though she now tells us that electing Ronald Reagan was a crime. (Diane recently wrote a letter asking in a rhetorical manner what happened to the generation of the 1968 barricades. She is referring to the Paris riots. Unfortunately for her she includes herself in that generation. Even more unfortunate for her is the fact that I remember what she did during the time of the barricades. She drove with me to Geneva because Regine's had closed down and she needed to hook her future husband. So much for the angry young woman.) Let me also add Kate Millet, Shirley Chisholm, Barbra Streisand. The list is endless.

But it is not long enough. The more I think on it the longer the list becomes. But not long enough to prevent the American male from making a comeback. All he has to do is try to behave a bit more like his ancestor, the macaque. Put the little woman on a pedestal, spoil her by protecting her, not by taking any back talk. Oppress her. She'll love it. Force her to be obedient and feminine and even her genetic traits will start responding again. That will bring her instant happiness. Even the bills will be reduced, what without valium to buy and shrinks to pay. Be jealous. Nothing works like a little bit of jealousy to bolster the female ego.

Finally, never be brutal, but be very firm. The Japanese beat their wives symbolically every day on the assumption that even if they don't know why they do it, their wives will understand. Japanese women — with the exception of Yoko Ono — have always been extremely happy. Let's take an example from the land of the rising sun. If Detroit had we wouldn't be in the economic mess we're in today. Ditto where sex is concerned. And I know that Americans prefer sex to cars.

WOMEN'S RITES: *Jeffrey Bernard*

I was sitting in Sagne's coffee shop in Marylebone High Street the other day watching Bernard Levin stuffing cream cakes into an expensive looking attaché case which already contained a fat biography of Pablo Casals, and I was thinking what a nice, well-kept, inoffensive, clean-cut man Mr Levin looked, though God knows he'd probably grab you by the throat if you were mad enough to cry out that you thought Richard Wagner must have been a soppy, self-indulgent, crumpet-struck, sentimental, fascist of a man, and it occurred to me that if I were as famous and clever as Mr Levin, although come to think of it famous by itself would probably do, then I'd have women eating out of my hands, which is the terminus for most of my trains of thought.

Mind you, in some ways I wouldn't think much of a woman who could lower herself to eat out of my hands, nevertheless I find it slightly irritating to think that the vast majority of women have no desire or intention to eat out of my hands, which I suppose could be called wanting my cake but not wanting to eat it. Anyway, Mr Levin left his box of treasures and just as my fantasy about him and his destination was getting cosy, and which concerned an Eleanor Bron-type woman in a flat around the corner furnished impeccably with expensive Victoriana and with a herb garden on the window ledge and a signed photograph of Ivy Compton Burnett next to the Victrola, just as I was thinking about that and just as Mr Levin, sitting at a decent distance from his lady on a chaise longue, had opened his musical snuff box which played *Liebestod* from *Tristan* this girl sitting opposite me opened her big mouth and said: 'I suppose you know that the Women's Lib movement is holding an international convention in Mexico City later this year?' Well no, I didn't, and I'm sorry to say that the statement broke my train of thought just as it had got to a good bit where Miss Bron, now kneeling at Mr Levin's feet, had started to undo his spats.

A Woman's Lib convention in Mexico City! My mind began to boggle and I realised then as I do now that I'd give my testicles to be able to attend it and report on it. I pushed the protesting and meringue-sodden Mr Levin to the back of my mind and all at once I could hear the smashing of Tequila bottles, the fanfare of the paso doble and the roar of a thousand vibrators. I saw myself as a sort of kamikaze journalist and I realised that Burton's trip to Mecca had been a mere package holiday for one.

My train of thought sped on crashing through the red lights of conventional, liberal thinking. There I was in my hotel room in the Plaza del Something typing out my story on a Remington Noiseless, a cheroot stuck in my mouth at an aggressive angle and my strong hands looking bronzed against the virgin foolscap I was stuffing into the Remington in the manner of a man who knows what he's going to say, when they smashed down the door of my bedroom. They stood there snarling, six of them, a haggle of Women's Libbers. 'Let's get the pig,' screamed their leader, a woman with a crew cut and a copy of *Time Out* sticking out of her Gucci briefcase.

They tied me up, and being a gentleman I didn't resist. They read out the charges against me, hundreds of them, and I remember that one of them accused me of having said that I thought women had got sillier and sillier since Women's Lib had started. Later, just before I died in the arms of a male nurse, I managed to mutter: 'Tell Lord Thomson I tried.'

Phew. These daymares are really beginning to get me down. Sometimes I fear for my mind. Sometimes I find it's just all too much. Insanity is like VD: you catch it by going to bed with people, and in some ways I look forward to old age and to be being a poor man's Malcolm Muggeridge and enjoying all that celibacy, those nut cutlets and disgusting memories.

Meanwhile, sitting here in Sagne's wondering whether a second chocolate slice will utterly put off the girl whom I fancy and who is sitting opposite me, I ponder the state of women. I suppose that one of their biggest problems these days is treading the very thin border line between being nice, generous, giving girls and being scrubbers. The problems of being a female journalist must be even greater. There's all that, plus what do you write, especially when you need the money? Do you stick to things you're sincere about and end up writing the sort of shallow stuff that Katharine Whitehorn produced on alcoholism? Do you write things you don't believe in and end up like Irma Kurtz and produce a piece on sex being overrated and then another on how awful promiscuity is or do you end up doing countless interviews like the *Guardian* do with career women on the assumption that any career makes any woman interesting?

I do all three from time to time but nowadays I send the stuff in and don't deliver it since the level of hostility in offices, particularly those of women's magazines, has reached an all-time high. The *Radio Times* is a good example. It's not a woman's magazine of course but it's staffed almost entirely by girls. There's a 'Don't come near me or regard me as a sex object' wall of ice that goes up as you walk into the office.

Since the age of 14 I have dearly wanted to be regarded as a sex object. I am absolutely sick of being loved for my cooking, accurate seam bowling, ability to solve anagrams, mow lawns, mend fuses and obtain credit from bookmakers and yet there are women who profess to be fearful of the alternative. Only last week I was suggesting to the editor of a woman's magazine that she should commission a piece from a man on the subject of some of the little problems involved in being a man like the fact that you're dead if you aren't successful, handsome, rich, reliable, dependable, strong, virile, and very clever. She said: 'I'm sorry. This is a woman's magazine and we're only interested in women's problems.' All right, so it wasn't a marvellous idea, but what an answer.

It got my mind boggling again. I could almost taste the sour grapes. There was Bernard Levin sitting by the side of a swimming pool in Mexico City, a chocolate éclair in one hand, a biography of Mozart in the other, typing a *Times* column with his right foot and surrounded by 16 girls he'd just converted from Women's Lib to the Let's be Nice to Men Organisation and I was watching it all from a tumbril on my way to a scaffold surrounded by old women clattering away at typewriters. Irma Kurtz was reporting the executions of male chauvinist pigs for *Cosmopolitan* and had a ringside seat, and next to her Katharine Whitehorn was beginning an in-depth piece for the *Observer* called 'Vasectomy: A Half Measure'.

The thing is I'd really very much like to report this Woman's

Lib convention if it is taking place but I can't think of an editor in London whom I could talk into letting me do it. The trouble is they're all of them only interested in women's problems.

POINTS OF STYLE: *Taki*

New York

It is typical of the world without style in which we live that the President of supposedly the most powerful nation in the world has to take personality lessons from Gerald Rafshoon, a man who can only be described, for lack of a better word, as the archetypal sleight-of-hand charlatan that Madison Avenue produces as abundantly as the PLO creates terrorists. Until President Carter's recent speech, in which he displayed the latest Rafshoonisms — clasped hands to convey togetherness, clenched fist to portray strength and decisiveness — Rafshoon's greatest contribution to the peanut farmer's image was to change the parting of Carter's hair from the right side to the left.

Although the President asked that all Americans unite in these difficult times, the consensus of opinion is that the only uniting the citizens are doing is behind the idea that never has an American President had less style than this Georgian. The last one to have some style was J.F. Kennedy: it was mostly the sartorial kind, but nevertheless there it was. After JFK the fortunes of America went quickly downhill. It doesn't take the opportunistic kind of thinking a poltroon like Arthur Schlesinger is bandying around to realise why. Style is as important as intellect when it comes to leading the free world. As long as we have American movies, television shows and culture to show us the way, style will be the most important element in getting elected — and re-elected. Which brings us back to Rafshoon and his kind.

But it wasn't always like that. There were times when the only sure-fire way of ensuring success was to act contrary to the wishes of the majority. Salvador Dali insists that the masses are always wrong, and proves it mathematically. Most people have ugly faces, ugly houses, and uglier tastes. It is only the very few that do not, he says, and it has nothing to do with money or education. It has to do with style. Wittgenstein once said that he didn't care what he ate as long as it was always the same. The seventh Earl of Lucan practised what the Austrian philosopher preached. 'Lucky' Lucan might not have had the best taste where terminating a marriage was concerned, nor the best judgment, but his palate was beyond reproach.

Here in the United States there is an obvious lack of style, and in one or two respects England is not far behind. For example, the 'groupie' phenomenon. Everyone here is a groupie: that is why America's number one booster of socialism, egalitarianism and an end to hypocrisy in high places, is a millionaire economist and *bon vivant* who winters in Gstaad among the beautiful people, the rich and the powerful. I am talking about Professor J.K. Galbraith, the man who has been more consistently wrong in his forecasts than the British weatherman. Nevertheless, when the avuncular Canadian, whose physical attributes make him the ideal man to clean giraffe ears, crosses Fifth or Park Avenue on his way to a chic cocktail party, the *hoi polloi* lets out the kind of screams reserved for lead guitarists.

Fonda, Lillian Hellman, the Berrigan brothers, Shirley Maclaine, the list is endless. They are all super-stars with one thing in common: a singular lack of style, and a double standard where politics are concerned. Style is the opposite of pretence. Theirs is pretence *tout court*. Churchill was innately vulgar, with his constant cigar-smoking, drinking and petty nastiness. Yet his force and deep commitment made him a man of great style. Today no politician has style, anywhere in the Western world.

CHANGE OF LIFE: *Jeffrey Bernard*

My man in Long Island has sent me an extraordinary story about a woman who says she can't survive on a half-million dollars a year. Our hearts must, at this time, go out to the dreadful woman. She goes by the name of Laura Steinberg and she has to live in the three-bedroom suite once occupied by President Nixon in the Hotel Pierre for which she pays $1,000 a day. Furthermore, she has to make do on a lousy $120,000 a year plus $700,000 worth of stocks. Added to which — wait for it — she doesn't even like the food at the Pierre. She is the estranged wife of tycoon Saul Steinberg who owns, amongst other things, the Rothschild Banks in Europe.

Anyway, Mrs Steinberg went to the Manhattan Supreme Court a little while ago to describe her terrible plight to a judge. She told him that her standard of living is extraordinarily high and that even under the present agreement she couldn't possibly afford what she'd become accustomed to. She walked out on the old man a couple of months ago, wants to come back, but he doesn't want her living in his place.

Now, if you're not already crying, I must hasten to add that she also claims her son needs a home. The little brat, she says, 'is vomiting in the hotel because he can't stand the food'. It's doubtful whether the Hotel Pierre has ever before had any complaints about the cuisine and if I was the manager, René Sauthier, I think I'd flog young master Steinberg within an inch of his wretched life with a Sole Bonne Femme and then hold his head in a Summer Pudding till he choked.

Mrs Steinberg also has the gall to claim that one of the troubles with her husband is that he doens't want to change his way of life. Surprise, surprise. Had I myself got $100 million I probably wouldn't want to change mine either. She also says that her husband beat her up several times over the years and I suspect that Bill Whelan, my man in Long Island, has probably hit the nail, if not Mrs Steinberg, on the head when he somewhat cynically suggests, 'Yeah, with a cheque book.'

If only Mrs Steinberg were English. We in this country know all about how tough it is at the top, and who on earth else in the world could have such a thing as The Distressed Gentlefolks Association? I will have you know, Mr Whelan, that there is a man a couple of miles from me who is roughing it on a par with your Mrs Steinberg. He's got his own few million; his wife, the daughter of a brewing tycoon, has even more but she decided it was high time they economise. 'One of the butlers will have to go,' she told him. He staggered back with shock and said, 'But who's going to put the lemon in the gin and tonic?' My friend the trainer, Antony Johnson, has some pretty good throwaway lines too. The other day, when I was looking for somewhere to throw my cigarette end, I spotted an objet d'art and asked him, 'Is this an ashtray or a priceless antique?' 'Both,' he said. I have only seen him visibly moved once, apart from the time he rescued my wife from the Caribbean, and that was when the Rolls Royce had the bad taste to acquire a puncture.

The likes of Mrs Steinberg should learn to keep a stiff upper lip in the face of adversity as having only a thousand dollars a day and I suggest, Mr Whelan, that you send her over here where, for a modest sum, I could give her one of my crash courses in survival. This consists of an exercise known as keeping the head above water. We start at 11 a.m. in the American bar of the Savoy with a couple of whisky sours. Now since we've only got £5 to kick off with, this leaves us very nearly skint. We take what little there is left to the nearest fruit machine and win the jackpot. We take the jackpot down the road to Sandown Park and back all six winners. Returning to town we dine on the sort of food that would make Steinberg junior puke. Say the Connaught. Then we go to a casino and gamble into the early hours. Dawn sees us holding a glass of Dom Perignon in one hand and £10,000 in the other. We do this at least twice a week and I'm getting pretty sick of it.

But please keep in touch, Mr Whelan. I am coming to the USA in a month and I'd very much like you to introduce me to some fellow sufferers in Manhattan.

BEYOND A JOKE: *Taki*

With the exception of Mr Nobel, despite his eventual act of contrition, no-one loved explosives more than Prince Victor Emmanuel of Savoy, son and heir of Italy's last king, Umberto. At a very young age he used them to blow up Le Rosey School's focal point and main campus attraction, a 500-year-old fountain. And although Le Rosey was known for catering to royal whims, so loud was the bang that the crown prince was sacked. The school, local press and Swiss authorities hushed up the incident at the time. Not out of consideration to the Italian royal family, nor because of the age of the culprit. Simply out of embarrassment. After all, how does one explain a fifteen-year-old getting hold of and transporting enough dynamite to blow up a stone well?

Twenty-five years later neither the authorities nor the newspapers are as shy. Perhaps because the crime is hardly that of a schoolboy prank. A nineteen-year-old German boy has lost his leg and almost his life because of the Prince's propensity for firearms.

Victor and his sisters grew up with little money but surrounded by social-climbing millionaires. They were, naturally, spoilt as well as impressed by the root of all evil. Nevertheless, Victor put his love of firearms to good use while becoming a helicopter and arms salesman for various companies. Because of his position every Arab and third-world country's doors were open to him. In ten years he became a multi-millionaire.

His choice of friends, and the company he kept, however, was not as impressive as his business acumen. In fact it was downright humiliating: there were playboys like Gunther Sachs, some Italian card hustlers and a few bike cowboys posing as easy riders. In 1968 I was present when Victor and his friend 'Charlie' Burundi, the Crown Prince of Burundi, later killed by radical pygmies, got into a drunken argument about how fast a Ferrari could go. Victor pulled a gun, and being an expert marksman, put a bullet very near Charlie's head. Everyone collapsed laughing, most of all Charlie.

There were other incidents involving guns. Victor married a Swiss girl, Marina Doria, known for her capacious mammary glands and zest for nightclub brawls. She once went too far with an admirer and Victor pulled a William Tell on her. Everyone laughed, most of all Marina.

Unable to go to Italy because of his position, Victor kept a summer home on the southernmost tip of Corsica, Cavallo, only a few hundred yards from Sardinia. He owned a Riva 42, an Italian-built cabin cruiser, which he kept docked in his little harbour in front of his house.

Recently a bunch of Italian playboys, headed by a Milanese named Nicola Penda, sailed to Cavallo from the Aga Khan's expensive little resort of Porto Cervo. Deciding to have some fun at Victor's expense they boarded his boat and stole his dinghy. Victor protested and got dunked for his troubles. Furious he went to the house, took out an M-16 carbine and fired over their heads.

Now an M-16 is a pretty lethal weapon. Its velocity and range are superior to any other weapon in existence. Purposely shooting away from them, Victor hit a boat lying far away in the distance. The bullet went through a bulkhead and almost severed the leg of a young man just above the thigh.

Dirk Hamer remained between life and death for two weeks. His leg was amputated as well as other things. His family went on Swiss television and very bravely stated that they knew it was an accident. They also told of their son's aptitude for sports. They, at the time of writing, have refused to press charges.

Victor has been languishing in a nine by ten-foot Corsican prison cell since. He is charged with assault and illegal possession of firearms. He claims that the M-16 was to defend himself against terrorist attacks. In this I believe him. What I also believe is that the Corsicans will make an example of him.

Given the enormity of his negligence Victor can hardly sleep peacefully the rest of his life. It was also typical of the Italian playboys to choose what they thought was an easy target. According to a witness they thought he was a fool. Little did they know how much of one.

THE BIG SLEEP: *Jeffrey Bernard*

Did you read or hear about the man who killed himself while trying to commit suicide the other day? Apparently this man, in an attempt to hang himself, climbed up a tree to attach a rope on to a branch and fell and broke his neck. Then there was the drunken motorist who was stopped by the police who asked him to take a breathaliser test. He ran away from them and inadvertently fell over a cliff, killing himself. A little longer ago, I'm told that the fire brigade were called out to rescue a kitten which had got stuck up a tree. They successfully rescued the animal, bringing him down to earth, and then the fire engine reversed over pussy, finally flattening him. Delightful stuff. Father Time must surely be about to join the great band of the unemployed. It makes one realise how delightfully uncomplicated lemmings are.

What worries me though is the amount of people who are making no attempt whatsoever to kill themselves when it should be, of course, their priority. I myself have to own up to a certain amount of lethargy concerning my own suicide which seems to be taking an age, but then I always did like to take things easily. Falling out of trees, over cliffs and beneath fire engines is far too sudden for me. I think though that Ruby is slowly talking me to death.

Ruby is a local barmaid who some call 'nurse'. She's middle aged, looks rather like Harpo Marx and she gets a taxi to and from work although she only earns £1 an hour. She lives on Bounty Bars and crisps — don't they all? — and she moans from opening time till closing time. I say she's talking me to death since I actually fell asleep at 11 a.m. the other morning when she was on at me, and I wasn't even tired. Does the tsetse fly lurk in Lambourn? Half an hour later I actually dozed off while standing in a queue in the dry cleaning shop. The women ahead of me spent 20 minutes discussing their forthcoming coffee morning and all of them with those fixed benign smiles on their faces just like Ruby has. I suddenly realised that I'm hypnotised by them and that's why I keep dropping off.

It's very odd. You know the way girls up till the age of 20 or so can't help giggling all the time, well, women who don't feel they're in direct competition with men, that is, housewives who've suffered brain damage from having been married to boring men for too long, they plod through life with the fixed smile. Age silences the giggle and then the paralysis of the smile sets in. There are men too in the Lambourn valley who can play the sandman just as effectively. I came closer to the grim reaper than I've ever been before the other day when a relative of Ruby's got me nodding off at a table in the pub car park. This is what I get a hell of a lot of.

'Plenty of work about for you Jeff? No? I should have thought you'd be doing very well. But it's the same for all of us really, isn't it? And, you mark my words, it's going to get a lot worse before it gets better. I mean there just isn't the money about is there? Mind you, it's alright for some I dare say; farmers and suchlike. No, when you think what a pound's worth today, well. Funny though, I should have thought those magazines and things you write for, I should have thought they'd pay very well. No? Of course, you know what you ought to do? I'll tell you. You should write a book. I'll tell you what. If I could write I'd sit down and write a book: God, the stories I could tell. Still, Fleet Street's cutting its own throat isn't it? I'll say one thing for Mrs Thatcher though, she's nobody's fool. Tell me, Jeff, what do you think of her? Oh you don't. Well we're all entitled to our views aren't we. One man's meat and all that. Oh well I suppose we'd better have one for the road, eh. Your usual I take it? Righty ho. By the way, Jeff, something I've always meant to ask you. You've met Lester Piggott haven't you? What's he *really* like?'

Now a few months ago, at this point, I would have simply screamed with the pain of it. But, this time, I fell asleep again. I'm beginning to think that off a tree, over a cliff or under a fire engine would be preferable after all.

DIPLOMACY: *Taki*

The flight from London to Athens was rather uneventful except for proletarian noises from the back of the aircraft and the slurping noises from a fat Greek businessman or government official in the first class section — where I was sitting. Fat Greek businessmen and government officials always make a lot of noise when they eat. I have never found one who didn't. Perhaps it is their way of attracting attention. This particular man, however, was overdoing it. I was sitting two rows away and could not concentrate on the book which I always read when flying, *Mein Kampf*. I complained to the British stewardess about the noise but to no avail. So finally I yelled abuse at him in Greek. That proved to be unwise, because the fat little creep got out of his seat and informed me that he was a government official and would see to it that I would pay for my rudeness. When I informed him that I had never suspected him of being anything but what he claimed to be, he became even crosser. But as British Airways do not teach their girls Greek, he couldn't make the stewardess understand so he sat and fumed for the whole journey while I kept glancing up from the Fuehrer's writings and winking at him.

Once on the ground, he immediately summoned a minion and started pointing in my direction. But it was not his day. My close friend Mr X, a top policeman of the Athens anti-terrorist squad, happened to be at the terminal. Mr X is not very popular with the Greek Left because he occasionally makes his opinions known about communism, atheism, and children who don't respect their parents and teachers. So we threw ourselves into each others' arms. When the minion came up to question me, my friend told him that he and his fat sponsor might be taken in for questioning because they were distracting a great writer who needed to think. He fled in terror. But unfortunately he had revealed my name to the slurper, so now I have one more mortal enemy in the birth-place of democracy.

But that is not all. Only one hour after I set foot in the birth-place of Alcibiades I was involved in another diplomatic incident. Going into my father's office to say Hello, I noticed a large photograph of Leonid Brezhnev with an inscription on it saying how much he loved and respected my shipowning Daddy. My father was not there, so I began to rip up the picture, shouting to his secretary that this was treason of the worst kind. At that point, my father entered the room in the company of a high Russian official who had just delivered the photographs. The Russian swallowed hard, turned bright red and started to make slurping noises à la grecque. My father, still unaware of my vandalism, proudly introduced him. Then he too turned red and began to scream. I left in a hurry, claim-ing to have eaten something poisonous on the plane.

As things stand, nobody in my family is speaking to me. My

father continues to spend his days with the Russian Ambassador and other high Soviet officials, while Mr X has informed me that in view of my father's recent friendships, ours must cease. With Easter, the holiest of Greek Orthodox days, at hand, I am alone and abandoned by everyone.

9. THE SPORTING LIFE: *Taki*

FAIR PLAY

The title 'high life' is misleading as I suddenly hit a snag in the pursuit of the good life. The reasons are simple. I went to Yugoslavia, for sport. Never again.

My odyssey began when selected to represent Greece as a contestant in the European karate championships held this year in Belgrade.

There were five other mental patients who made up the team plus some accompanying journalists. The latter were invited by the Yugoslav government.

Our hotel could have been worse. Although it had cockroaches I never during one week there saw a large rat. Nor did anyone die of food poisoning despite the fact that everyone got sick. But to describe peeling plaster, broken sinks, the smell of urine and general shabbiness is not the purpose of this column. Suffice it to say that it resembled a Cuban whorehouse on a pre-Castro Sunday morning.

One forgot these petty problems, however, when confronted with the human factor, especially the staff. To describe them would be plagiarism. They were already characterised in Solzhenitsyn's Gulag trilogy. One need simply substitute the word 'waiter' for 'guard'.

On Friday evening delegations from the seventeen competing nations were summoned to a showplace congress hall for the annual elections. Nine votes went to the English candidate for president of the Karate Federation, seven to the Yugoslav while Belgium abstained.

Because of the abstention the Yugoslavs decreed the vote null and void. We voted again. This time the Englishman got ten votes to the Yugoslav's seven. But again he was not elected. It seems that he did not have enough of a majority, according to the Yugoslavs. We then spent four hours arguing the definition of the word 'majority'. Finally the Englishman resigned and the Yugoslav became president.

The tournament started fast and furious on Saturday morning. By a lucky coincidence Yugoslavia passed the first two rounds on byes and was on the easy side of the draw. Powerful England by an unlucky coincidence was on the other side along with the rest of the good teams. But a word about competition karate first.

Karate was originally an empty-handed art of self defence in which arms and legs were systematically trained to be used as weapons. The essence of the martial art was *kime*, or the focus of strength. A sudden explosion of technique coupled with speed producing power.

The first purpose of the art was the nurturing of a sublime spirit, the spirit of humility through strength. But with the passing of the Samurai, or Bushido philosophy, and the coming of materialism and the American occupation forces, karate changed. There had to be competitions because in America there are lists of who is better. So competition karate began. Under the rules, the line between disqualification and victory is very thin.

The crowds packing the vast indoor stadium were an exact replica of those that used to go to Nuremberg rallies, except for the uniforms, but just as lobotomised and loud. We fought Hungary first. The crowd was for them for some strange reason. Four of us were disqualified for excessive contact. The Hungarians made up for what they lacked in fighting spirit by their Thespian abilities. They took more dives screaming in pain than Italian footballers.

In the meantime Yugoslavia murdered her opponents but because of a lucky coincidence in judging she was not disqualified. She won the team competition. Some things did not go as planned. An Englishman won despite the fact that most of his teammates were either disqualified or put to fight each other. (The English are the best in Europe.)

By accident Wales was denied a flag during the ceremonies. But it was no accident when I gave a two-fingered sign to the officials after my last match and was banned from further competition in Yugoslavia.

AMATEURS

Despite some ugly rumours that I was never at Eton, spread I am sure by envious people who went to lesser schools, I returned to my Alma Mater last weekend to watch the world championship racquets final. And I saw the fastest racquet game in the world played by four rather strange young men. I say strange because, unlike their tennis counterparts playing somewhere in Baron's Court, the racquets players did not wear cretinous smirks worthy of Iranian and Libyan diplomats, nor did their prize money challenge Russia's defence expenditure. There were no tantrums, no ego trips, no swearing; enough to make any McEnroe or Connors groupie freak out. Willie Boone, a land surveyor, and my old friend Randall Crawley, an art dealer, whose combined income is probably one hundredth of Borg's, beat Howard Angus and Andrew Milne, two gentlemen who wouldn't be considered rich even in Albania.

I mention money because, although it sounds rather vulgar, it is, alas, important. Plebians believe that amateur sport is a pastime for the rich. Yet they are wrong. Amateur sport is not expensive and it is, I have always found, much more competitive than professional sport. Although amateur tennis players used to compete for very little prize money, it was pride and nothing else that spurred them on. On average today's standard is much higher. But I still feel, when I see some of the superstars, as if I were watching Cyril Stein competing with Victor Lownes for petro-dollars. This is different from the kind of eager gallantry that is shown by Eton sixth-formers.

All this reminds me of a match I played once. It was at Bristol, about 15 years ago, two weeks before Wimbledon. I had just arrived from Paris and gone straight on to a grass

court to play against an unknown, Gerald Battrick. He was a
snooty, smart-assed type, with an unpleasant face and an
awkward type of game. He won the first set, and I was furious,
thinking I was about to lose to a county player. So I tried to
like hell and won the second. Then he became furious, thinking
that he would lose to the worst player on the circuit. After
some questionable calls from both sides (there were no
referees in those days for first round matches; as there was
no money involved, no one really cheated), he won the third,
The lack of financial incentive did nothing to diminish the heat
of the contest.

Tennis did not become an economic phenomenon until the
Seventies. The romantic idea of amateur sport, however sham,
was discarded in 1970 and with it went what used to be called
style. In its place came greasy hair, worn long like footballers
and constantly brushed out of the eyes, synthetic, poly-
chromatic garments to make up for the loss or rather lack of
personality. And hexagonal rackets, plastic fibre or metal
ones, even one with a giant head that guarantees to stop
miss-hits

Given all the changes that tennis has endured, it would be
abnormal, even for Wimbledon, not to be affected. And the
willingness of Wimbledon enthusiasts to accept almost anything helped the transition. Where once there were high teas
and strawberries there are now hamburgers and hot dogs,
strawberries in disposable cartons and pizzas in plastic boxes.
Pretty soon some enterprising Cypriot will open a souvlaki
stand near court fourteen.

The social level of the spectators has gone down too.
Formerly they were neatly dressed and school girls wore
boaters and uniforms. And fainting at the sight of John
Lloyd's legs (whose agent, by the way, has shrewdly exploited
the press's fascination with them. Not since Betty Grable has
so much been written about a pair of legs. Nastase's agent
told me, in a fit of jealousy, that he hopes Lloyd gets varicose
veins.)

Agents are a proliferating species in Wimbledon during the
championships. Just before playing Chris Evert on Tuesday,
Billie-Jean King announced that she was setting up the

International Management Group. The announcement spread
around the locker rooms like wildfire. Agents and PR men
cajoled, threatened or begged players for a commitment.
Where once Emerson sang a high falsetto in the showers,
and Pietrangeli bragged about girls, you now hear things like
'I am out of commodities as of today', or 'Yen, buy yen and
short the mark.'

INDOOR SPORTS

The most titillating three-letter word in the English language
is one and the same with the most controversial word in sport.
Sex. Since time immemorial, or as long as men and women
have engaged in competitive sports, arguments have raged
over whether or not sexual activity hinders athletic performances. I have always thought the contrary. The greatest
athletes in the world were what a disgusting publication like
Playboy calls swingers. Jim Thorpe, the legendary Indian who
probably was the greatest all-around athlete of all time, did
not, I believe, compete once after the age of 18 without a
terrible hangover. And everyone knows that where there is a
hangover there has been sex.

Babe Ruth, the greatest baseball player of all time, was
another example. The Babe was as legendary a drinker as he
was a woman-chaser. He is the one that made the saying
'it's not fucking that ages you but chasing after it' popular.
His manager on the New York Yankees, Miller Huggins, could
not understand why Babe looked so haggard every morning.
He asked Babe to level with him, assuring him his revelations
would not be held against him. After all, Babe was the leading
home-run hitter in baseball. When he heard the Babe's
schedule Huggins cringed. 'You mean you spend from 8 in
the evening until 4.30 in the morning working to have pleasure
for only two minutes?' he asked.

Ironically, it explains many athletes' ability to perform as
well on the field as they do badly in bed. As Billie-Jean King
said in her inimitably vulgar manner, 'All you want to do is
activate all the centres. It's the three-hour sessions that
kill you.' Sexual relations on the night before competition do

not hinder athletic performance, provided that sex is a regular part of the athlete's life. Take another example. Lennard Bergelin, Swedish tennis champion during the early Fifties, and now Bjorn Borg's coach and one of the reasons for Borg's success, was, like most Swedes, a pretty cold fish but before each important match he would insist on having sex.

Philippe Washer was probably the most talented tennis player in Europe during the late Forties and early Fifties. He was also a scratch golfer and top skier. Good-looking and filthy rich, Washer had no trouble attracting the weaker sex. Washer indulged constantly and was successful on both fields. Except when playing against Bergelin. Against the Swede Philippe would abstain. And invariably lose. One day Bergelin told him to try his method. Washer did, after having abstained all week, and killed the Swede. But the trick only worked against Lennard Bergelin. When Washer abstained during the week and indulged just before the match against others he would do badly. He got prematurely old worrying about it. And never figured it out.

Nor have the doctors. They have been studying the subject ever since the Ancient Greeks inquired whether having one's student before the marathon was OK, but have been unable to prove that sex and sport do not mix. Yet every coach in the world will swear that they don't. Ken Norton, the boxer who actually beat Mohammed Ali, in my opinion, all three times he fought him, claims that he gave up sex for eight weeks before fighting Ali. The only wonder is that he didn't try to kiss him in the clinches. Yet Norton insists that, 'a couple of times during my first ten or eleven fights I didn't abstain and it hurt me.'

Dwight Stones, who once broke two world records in the high jump admitted he had had sex only two hours before setting the record. Some wags said it made him lighter. But it was Suzy Chaffee, the American Olympic skier and alleged girlfriend of Teddy Kennedy who is the greatest exponent of sex before competition. 'Too much accumulated energy can work against you,' she says. Although not an athlete, Kennedy seems to agree.

FAMOUS VICTORY

It was the greatest victory of good over evil since John Wayne carried the day for the marines in *Sands of Iwo Jima*. Or Gary Cooper survived the final shoot out in *High Noon*. Here was Pat Dupré a 24-year-old Stanford University student, down one set and 0-4 in the second, only to rally and equalise by taking six games in a row. Then later, down two sets to one, he came back and won the match 6-3 in the final set. He did this against the all-Italian boy, Adriano Panatta.

Dupré has served seven double faults in the first set and had been swept off the Centre Court by the Italians. Yes, he was playing about 200 of them at the same time. Every waiter in Soho and the Fulham Road was there, their usual obnoxious selves. This time they weren't insulting English couples guilty of having chosen an Italian restaurant to have dinner, but a young unseeded American trying to make it into the semi-finals of the championships. They hooted, heckled,

harassed and downright hissed the few winners Dupré pulled off; they intimidated him and certainly helped Panatta to sail clear early on.

The Italian is a good player but I would say that if he didn't have his army behind him he would be 30-love less good. In Italy opponents are physically intimidated by flying objects, and linesmen cheat openly or because they fear for their lives. In Paris the same. There are waiters everywhere in Europe and all of them ready to go out and show the world, by helping Panatta win, that Italy's rather pathetic performance whenever a world war breaks out was an aberration.

The spaghetti brigade, however, could not intimidate the Wimbledon linesmen and referee. In any other country Dupré would have got bad calls during crucial points. Not here. It was nevertheless disgraceful to hear (and unfortunately) smell their garlic shouts in the staid and glorious old Centre Court.

Tennis, as everyone knows, is a very psychological game. There are times when a man gets his racquet back before the opponent's ball has crossed the net, steps in and reads what the ball has written on it although he knows damn well he is playing Dunlop or Slazenger. Then he follows through by almost pointing the racquet like a gun to where he wants the ball to go. That is what is called playing well. When smelly waiters shout and cheer your mistakes many players tend not to look closely if the ball says Slazenger on it, or get the racquet back before the ball has crossed the net.

Dupré, to his credit, shut his ears to the crowd by going back and concentrating just on the basics mentioned above. In the fifth set, as Dan Maskell said, it is character that wins. To arrive there usually means the two opponents are equal in ability. Dupré had character. Panatta, despite the help, did not. He is like the rest of his countrymen. Pretending to be bored when outrages are going on. He could easily silence the crowds in Rome, Paris, even Wimbledon by stating that their animal-like noises are hurting his game more than his opponent's. He chooses not to because their behaviour helps him win.

It's like chic Marxist professors in Italy. They were eager to encourage civil disobedience in order to seem attractive to the daughters of rich businessmen they were courting. Now the country has gone down Swanee because everyone thought it was such fun to see certain institutions, like the police or law and order, flouted.

Well, for once, England did something right. The people began cheering an American, of all people, and he in turn fought on because of the unfair behaviour of Panatta's supporters. The Italians had to go back to their restaurants and insult their customers once again. But they could not bask à la Philip Martyn and all the groupies in the world in his reflected glory. It was well worth having to smell them.

CHEAP THRILLS

Ed (Too Tall) Jones is a six foot nine inch, 270 pound negro who used to make £60,000 per year knocking people down. Jones did this legally as he played in defence for the Dallas Cowboys, an American football team. In American football, a defending player is usually black, very large, extremely tough, unusually mean and encouraged by the rules to use his hands, elbows, shoulders, even his head in order to remove immovable objects preventing him from reaching his objective, the quarter-back, who is usually white, unusually smart and much better paid than the defender.

This year, at 29 years of age, Jones suddenly announced his retirement and declared that he was turning in his shoulder pads and helmet for a pair of eight ounce gloves. He also announced that he was going to be the next heavyweight champion of the world. The Dallas fans screamed 'Say it ain't so Ed', the sportswriters laughed, and the Cowboys' front office executives just shook their heads and said it was another ploy by Jones's agent to extract more money from them. As it turned out everybody was wrong. Well, almost wrong.

Too Tall did quit for more money but not Cowboy money. It seems that someone by the name of David Wolf, whose greatest achievement up to date has been to write a book about a basketball player, connived with the Columbia Broadcasting System in order to hoodwink the great American public into believing that Too Tall could fight. CBS, as if one didn't know, is William Paley's £1000 million conglomerate, a company which has contributed uniquely to the turning of Americans into robot-like humanoids that emit commercial-like noises every three minutes. (A well respected man I know, a captain of industry no less, frequently goes off at a tangent: 'Do you suffer from painful haemorroids?' he says, 'then try new, improved Preparation H.' The man, like every other American, watches a lot of TV, and has replaced the talking and thinking process by commercials. CBS has a programme called *The Sports Spectacular*, an event unequalled to date in bad taste and false expectation. Things like wrestling cheer leaders, underwater weightlifting by midgets, and demolition derbys by paraplegics are not beyond the realm of the producer's imagination. In fact it is the ultimate in pornography, if one subscribes to the belief that having seen everything as far as sex is concerned, the only thing left that still excites is violence.

The plebian Paley is considered a great American aristocrat. He buys a lot of fancy objects and owns great houses. He has also been selling cheap programmes to the American consumer for the better part of 30 years. Last week Paley's little conglomerate brought Too Tall's fight into our living rooms in living colour. Jones's opponent was a man called Yacqui Meneses who had skin which in boxing parlance is described as being of the caucasian persuasion. Meneses, it turned out, was part white, part Indian, part Chinese, which ensured the ethnic audience, and in turn made CBS a fortune from sponsors like Budweiser Beer and Preparation H.

There was only one problem. For the future that is. Too Tall knew as much about boxing as Pol Pot and Khomeini know about compassion. The white, red, yellow man ran away for five rounds but in the sixth, Meneses got inside a runaway right lead and left-hooked Too Tall by jumping up while holding his trousers with one hand for leverage. Jones collapsed and was being counted out when, for some inexplicable reason, Meneses pushed the counting ref aside and punched down the prostrated and dreaming Too Tall. That, of course, disqualified the white, yellow, red kid and now Too Tall can continue his schedule of 42 bouts over the next 30 months.

There is nothing surprising about this. Managers like Wolf have wolf-like appetites and do not mind spilling blood, as long as it's not theirs but that of their boys. What is surprising is that CBS will televise his next fight. I wonder if they can get the next boxer to disqualify himself if by an accident he happens to make contact with Too Tall's chin? Whatever the case, the only man Too Tall should be allowed to fight is Bill Paley. It would be advertised as the battle of the tallest against the greediest. It would be a sellout.

10. AT THE RACES: *Jeffrey Bernard*

HOOKED

Last Saturday I took my ten-year-old daughter to Ascot Races. It was the first time I had seen her for nine months, for one reason and another, and it was a sheer delight to be seen with her. She is still very much on the leg and obviously needs time but she has tremendous scope and is very much on the upgrade. She has a dark bay mane of hair and an attractive head and eye and if she ever gets put out to grass then my name isn't what it is. But it was a rather bizarre day. She met a whole wad of the notables of the fraternity, saw the epic race between Known Fact and Kris and ended the day in the Owners' and Trainers' bar being kissed by Joe Mercer while she clutched a tiny purse swollen with £25. What the form experts would call a gentle introduction to the game, don't you think? But I wasn't very pleased about the money aspect really and I'm not sure that it isn't a little patronising to give small girls money and so much more than they're used to. My fault really. I should have stopped them.

What happened was that as soon as we arrived on the course one of the 'faces' pressed £2 into her hand. She looked rather embarrassed. Half an hour later, a rich owner pushed no less than £10 at her and said, 'Back my horse in the next race.' Far too much, but I put it on for her and we watched the horse fail by half a length and the same again. A close up third. For a moment I thought a tear might spill over and I hurriedly delivered the lecture about learning how to lose and not to

123

believe too much in magic. She seemed to get the message and I continued my guided tour of the racecourse.

I think she was obviously puzzled by the contrast between the time which it takes to run a race and the time that one spends propping up bars. The first is over in a flash of sorts, but the crowded, smoke-filled bars full of scoundrels shrieking with laughter and falling over must seem like suffering insane hard labour to a schoolgirl; it amused me a little to see her trying to take the whole mad business in. Then another owner approached, was introduced, and he too put some money into her hand. By this time I was skint and I was seriously thinking of embezzling her loot. The thought of a *News of the World* headline reading 'Father Mugs Daughter' was too disgusting to contemplate though, so I put her fiver on the tip we got and it romped in by three lengths. Never have I seen such delight on a face. She now had £20 in the kitty while I was wondering if I could summon up the cheek to get a credit bet on and collect cash in the event of a win. That's a rather infra-dig way of punting but when needs must . . . Luckily, I did just about get out of trouble and she won another five. 'What on earth are you going to do with so much money?' I asked her. 'Pay for some riding lessons,' she said. I was about to deliver her a few well chosen clichés, such as an idle mind being the playground of the devil, but as the great Joe Mercer removed his pipe from his mouth in order to bestow a kiss on her I thought it might be a little churlish. But she's definitely hooked.

GUILTY PARTY

Wasn't it Ivy Compton-Burnett who said that speculation means trying to make a great deal of money, and investment means trying to prevent a great deal of money becoming a small amount of money?

Actually, it wasn't. It was Fred Schwend, Jr.

What I'm trying to say is, can any speculating reader lend me £100 until the second Epsom meeting in May? It's a matter of life and misery. On 12 March, two horses, Attribute and

Cool Alibi, both of them white-hot favourites, were excused exercise for the day and sent to Hereford and Wetherby where they behaved like a couple of pigs and actually ran out. I could account for them being unaccountably last, but to run out, well, it's just the bloody end. Wasn't it Henry James who said, *C'est magnifique, mais ce n'est pas le course*? Actually, it wasn't. It was Cyril Stein when he went on a day trip to Boulogne. But the point is, I put more money on these two horses than I've ever staked in my life. I chased the losses, trebled them, and chased them again.

I was the last person in the betting shop that afternoon, and not being able to believe the results I stared at the board as though the writing would change if I stared long enough. As the clerks were locking up for the day, one of them said to me, 'Well, I will say, sir, you're a very good loser.'

'Aren't all losers good as far as you're concerned?' I asked him.

'Well, yes. But at least you smile, sir.'

'I'm not smiling,' I told him. 'My mouth's been stuck like this even since the 3.15.'

'I should go home and have a hot drink sir, if I were you,' he said, looking at a frayed *Sporting Life* twitching in my hand. Another ex-Air Raid Warden, I thought. Their cure for anything is a nice hot drink. But what I really wanted was to tell the bookmaker that it had all been a ghastly mistake, and persuade the stewards of the Jockey Club to re-run every event. I felt unbelievably sick, and started to crawl home to consult Edmund Bergler's *Psychology of Gambling* to see whether my neurosis centred around infantile omnipotence and its masochistic elaboration, or whether it resulted from guilt about Oedipal fantasies that were used to conceal a more deeply repressed guilt pertaining to the earlier oral level. Are you with me? Right. Quite obviously I was suffering from some unidentified guilt, and wanting to be objective about it I had decided to feel guilty about gambling. So between sobs I set about to do some psychological detective work. And what d'ya know? I felt guilty about not having any money and subconsciously thought that the easiest way to get some without actually getting dangerously near work was to back a few

horses. What's more, folks, thanks to Ed Bergler M.D. I've
found an absolutely 100 per cent, Ascot Gold Cup, stone bonk-
ing, racing certainty of a system. That's why I want to borrow
£100. You've all heard of beginner's luck? Well, the explan-
ation is quite simple. Some time must elapse before the
pleasure-pain cycle is completed, and punishment overtakes
the gambler for his masochistically tinged pseudo-aggression.
So, if we stop betting for long enough to make us beginners
when we do start again, and when we do start again we plunge
heavily on the worst bred, most inconsistent, uncourageous,
long shot in the race, we should collect before he has time to
realise that he should have run like a denying father figure.
It's easy, really. All you have to do is keep your head.

One man who kept his but probably drove his horses out of
theirs was the fourth Duke of Portland, who died in 1854.
Every day he had his horses ridden past a drum and fife band,
while men from his estate lined the route cheering and waving
flags. The Duke periodically let off fireworks in the stables to
make the horses unshockable, and they became so used to it
that they never flinched when he switched to pistols. Another
cool-headed customer was Lord George Bentinck who, when a
young man, lost £26,000 on the 1826 St Leger. He described
the incident as 'the most disastrous event of my racing life.'
His father had a poor opinion of gambling and gave him a
severe lecture on the subject and an estate in Scotland which,
it was hoped, was too far from a racecourse. A year later he
found the urge irresistible and began again. This time, as
insurance, he took his two brothers to Drummond's Bank
where they guaranteed him £300,000 whenever he wanted it.

A man who knew quite clearly in his mind the pitfalls of
racing was Mr Charles Greville. Most of us, at some time or
another, have hated some aspect of it, or have despised some
of its followers, and in 1838 Greville wrote in his diary 'Racing
is just like damn drinking, momentary excitement and
wretched intervals, full of consciousness of the mischievous
effects of the habit and equal difficulty in abstaining from it.'

In 1945 he added, 'These are my holidays, exclusively
devoted to the turf, passed in complete idleness, without
ever looking into a book, or doing one useful or profitable

thing, living with the merest wretches, whose sole and perpetual occupation it is, jockeys, trainers, bettors, blacklegs, people who do nothing but gamble, smoke and take everlastingly of horses.'

Mr George Payne sat up all night playing *écarté* with Lord Londesborough on the eve of his lordship's wedding, and left in the morning £30,000 to the bad. The eccentric fifth Earl of Glasgow hated naming his horses and gave them names like 'He does not deserve a name', 'Give him a name', and 'He has got a name now'. The earl also was fond of hunting his own huntsmen and shooting his keepers, and the endearing old gentleman set fire to the bedclothes of a club servant who went to bed before having served him a drink. He was very unlucky on the turf, but when a friend sympathised with him, he said 'No one is unlucky who has an income of £150,000 a year.'

Oddly enough, Edmund Bergler M.D. did not mention one of these rambling gambling men in *The Psychology of Gambling*. I've buried the volume in the garden alongside my guilt. And about that £100 I need. Next week will do.

EXCERPTS FROM COLONEL MAD

I and two of my field lieutenants were grossly insulted on Charisma Records day at Kempton Park recently. Attempting to converse with jockey Brian Smart, we were rudely interrupted by the heavy and utterly humourless Jenny Pitman who screamed out to Smart, 'Come away from those dreadful people. Anything you say will end up in *Private Eye*.' Her dour and equally humourless husband, who recently gained a 'A' Level in elocution and who rode unplaced in the Donkey Derby on Charisma Day, was elsewhere busy dropping aitches. I understand that they were picked up by Jimmy Lindley who has been using them to great effect on BBC. Should he, by any chance, eventually drop them I'd be grateful if they could be returned to Fred Winter from whence they originally came.

Newspaper stories about Lester Piggott missing death by inches at The Curragh on Irish Sweeps Derby day were a load of old balls. Pictures showed the wizened wizard curled up on the turf after baling out from Glencoe Lights at the end of the Sean Graham Sprint.

The story behind the picture — Lester landed awkwardly and damaged the contents of his jock strap. Later, when an Irish doctor remarked to him, 'You look a bit shaken up,' the maestro is reputed to have answered, 'So would you if you'd just fallen off a horse you'd had five grand on.'

This is obviously apocryphal since jockeys aren't allowed to bet.

Who should Colonel Mad come face to face with in a box at Ascot last Saturday but the ridiculous Peter Cundell. In an attempt to bury the hatchet that he's complained that I buried in his thick skull, I offered my congratulations on a recent winner he trained at Bath. Hazarding further light chat I added that I'd even backed it. The furious Cundell — in 'Saki's' immortal works, turning the colour of a beetroot who has just heard bad news — snarled, 'If I'd known that, I would have stopped it.' Ignoring this childish display of bad temper I asked Cundell to kindly remind me of the name of the horse in question. 'Look it up in the bloody form book,' he snapped. I've heard of late developers on the racecourse, but this is ridiculous. Mr Cundell will have to try and grow up, get out of nurseries and enter himself for a three-year-old event. His mumbled threats in and around Compton to actually punch Colonel Mad are also a trifle childish. Apart from anything else, Mad is far too old and weak to whack, and lists among his several complaints peripheral neuritis, delirium tremens, diabetes and an extremely useful minder.

I bumped into Ken Payne last week. He's running a hair-dressing establishment not a stone's throw from the Colonel's chambers near Baker Street. I gather the customers are looking very well turned out in spite of the fact that Monsier Payne is putting three under the same dryer at the same time. The staff had a teabreak two months ago.

I bought two books in error last week, *Nijinsky* and *The Art of Rigging*. One of them turned out to be the biography of a Russian poove and the other, which I thought to be a handbook on seamanship, is the biography of Cyril Stein.

Local News. Lambourn. Barry Hills, I'm told, has just bought an ice-chip making machine for £800 for use in cooling down the odd sore shin. This extravagant gesture was made, they say, because all the ice at Noel Bennet's pub is needed for Tony Stratton-Smith's flying visits. Since the machine was installed, Hills has been plagued by his head lad, Hughie Heeney, who follows him around the yard all day asking, 'Where the hell's the gin to go with the bloody ice?'

Lingfield. That go-ahead clerk of the course, John Hughes, the man who installed a £10,000 watering system at Chepstow racecourse some years ago in the shape of 10,000 watering cans at £1 each, has come up with another cracking idea, they tell me. Hot on the heels of his afternoon-cum-evening meeting he is putting on a morning meeting at Lingfield Park to be televised by Grampian and Tyne Tees Television. What will this toffee-nosed genius come up with next?

Somewhere in Berkshire. Michael Phillips, our man from *The Times*, is reported to have gone to a fancy dress party as Mrs Jean Hislop. When John Hislop asked him who he was supposed to be, and Phillips replied, 'Your wife', the breeding expert is supposed to have said, 'Don't be daft, you haven't got a treble gin in your hand.'

Seven Barrows. The deposed and smooth talking Danny Mellen, I hear, burst into Mr Walwyn's sitting room the other day and announced that he had cracked the employment problem. He has gone into the bloodstock agency business with his severance pay from William Hill — this should enable him to buy one leg of a two-year-old at Doncaster — and he will, in future, be known as Danny 'Rip Off' Mellen.

Great Shits of the British Turf: 1
CLEMENT FREUD

It is not without significance that Clement Freud, after one of
his unmemorable matches with Sir Hugh Fraser, collapsed in
the weighing room at Bath and was sick over very nearly
everything bar the Clerk of the Scales. This man is given to
uttering more bullshit re punting than anyone else on the Turf
except, possibly, Henry Alper — see Shits of the Year: 2 in
next issue. Undoubtedly one of the country's worst punters
and backgammon players, his presence on the QEII for the
backgammon championship of the world some time ago,
must have been for purposes of tax loss. When the competition
reached semi-final status, Freud advised Victor Lownes to
make Charles Benson the 9-2 outsider of the four remaining
players. His judgment cost Lownes £11,000. When Benson
pointed out the error of Freud's ways concerning this thinking
man's game, the pompous and hideous MP got on his high
horse and screamed, 'Do you realise you can't talk like that?
I've got parliamentary constituents and I'm here on my
merits!' When Benson got to the final he was approached by
Freud, his eyes full of tears, who then said: 'Help me. I didn't
think you played so much.' Unfortunately for all concerned,
the QEII was, at the time, making slow progress due to two
previously burst boilers, and the voyage lasted an extra day.
To while away the time, Freud suggested a consolation tournament. Phillip Martyn, who cost £1,500 in the auction pool, won
the contest and got knocked by the member for the Isle of Ely.
It is generally thought that Freud's appearance covers and
hides tremendous virtue of some sort or another. What it is
is yet another mystery of the Turf.

Soho. Michael Wale overcame his normal shyness with barmen by loudly ordering and paying for a round of drinks at
The Swiss Tavern in Old Compton Street, Soho. 'Enough's
enough,' screamed Wale, 'This'll prove I stand my round.'
'Michael,' said Tony Stratton-Smith, 'One swallow does not
make a summer.'

HER CHAMPAGNE

I'd got almost used to there being no racing during the spell
of bad weather and I was beginning to wonder what it was that
I missed most about it when it wasn't on the cards. The
resumption at Kempton Park brought it all back in every sort of
a way. Firstly, let it be said that Kempton Park is a dump
which is just a little better than no racing at all. I'm not
altogether sure why it should be so, but I think it's probably
because the place has less 'atmosphere' than any other track
and the grandstand is a kind of institutionalised building
half way between a hospital and a greyhound racing stadium.
Anyway, there it was, damp and bleak and embracing a gravel
pit and there she was in the owners' and trainers' bar —
legless, speechless and mindless. She is one of the country's
more successful owners. She wears angora jerseys that encase
the sort of tits you haven't seen since the fifties — torpedoes
— and she wears fur hats that make her look like a pantomime
rabbit.

It's always comforting to see a bigger idiot at the races
and, anyway, she's very good at pushing the boat out. As
soon as I'd put my head round the door, looking for a certain
trainer in fact and some information, she shouted, ''Allo
darling, come and have some champagne.' Now although
champagne isn't a very good mount to gin and tonic I had just
the one bottle to be sociable. She had a runner in the second
race, said she didn't fancy it and only had £100 each way to
prove it. Her husband must have been turning in his grave,
poor sod. Fancy being dead after all that hard work and
looking down, or up as the case may be, and seeing all that
hard earned loot frittered away on horses and bubbly. Never
mind. As I say, she's a lovable old boot and thinking just that
I was prompted to have a small bet on Bootlaces who duly
obliged at 10-1, although you could have got a little bit of 21-1
if you'd been paying attention.

Never mind, a winner's a winner and Kempton started
looking better with every move. So much so that after the last
race no one wanted to go home. The bar was packed until

dark and until the barmaids ran out of steam. There was one
fairly sensible interval in the lunacy when someone who'd
spent some time in Ireland recently sang the praises of Monks-
field loud and clear and said that we should all get on him for
the Champion Hurdle on 15 March. Earlier in the afternoon,
Richard Baerlein of the *Guardian* who actually knows what
he's talking about, was still very sweet on the chances of
another Irishman, Brown Lad, for the Gold Cup on 16 March.
He was particularly sweet on him in view of the atrocious
weather and we all know how Irish horses love the mud just as
the natives do. Perhaps a little each way double on the two
might show a profit.

The only other interesting and sober remark I heard during
the afternoon was made about Fred Winter's appalling run of
luck at Cheltenham over the past few years. This chap said
that it wasn't bad luck, but that Winter's horses were always
'over the top' by the time that Cheltenham came round. I'm
not sure quite what to make of that. It sounds a plausible
theory, on the other hand you might think Winter to be far too
shrewd a nut to allow that to happen.

After all this and that, Richard Hannon drove me to
Newbury in what seemed like five minutes. Racing people
do tend to drive like they bet. In Newbury I stayed the night
with Jimmy Lindley. Over breakfast the following morning and
while looking at an old form book, I remarked to him that 1963
and 1964 had been good years for him since he'd won the
2,000 Guineas with Only for Life and the St Leger on Indiana.
I was surprised when he said that they'd been bad years too.
He told me, 'For the sake of one and a half lengths, I lost
ten per cent of close on £1 million.' I asked him how and he
said, 'I got beaten half a length in the Derby, half a length in
the Arc de Triomphe and half a length in the Grand Prix de
Paris.'

What he didn't say though but proves he's a clever chap is
that he rightly decided *not* to become a trainer when he hung
the saddle up. Take a look around at the *flat* jockeys who turn
to training. They're, by and large, useless. The jump boys do
so much better. Winter, Rimell and Mellor, to name but three.
You wouldn't have sent a gift horse to Gordon Richards and

it's all very odd because he isn't exactly daft. Perhaps the jump people simply have better social connections and so manage to get some decent animals to care for. Whatever it is though isn't or wasn't apparent at Kempton Park. If you can actually manage to exist through a Saturday without going to the races, then I advise an avoidance of that place. It really is awful — apart from her and her champagne.

PUSSIES GALORE

I'm quite seriously worried about going mad. I don't think I could take another really bad winter without cracking at the seams and the long range weather men say that the athletes among us will soon be skating on the Thames. That thin dividing line that people are so fond of referring to, the one between sanity and insanity, was breached by three of us — in Battersea of all places — the last time we had a surfeit of snow and ice. What happened was that they had to cancel all racing for several weeks. Well, it might not have worried you much, but Caspar the diplomat, Tom the copywriter and myself never let work get in the way of racing in those days and we'd be punting from the first to last race every day.

But I'd better explain about Caspar because this is about him more than about Tom or me. He wasn't really a diplomat but he worked at a foreign embassy as a press officer and to hear him talk you'd think he ran the Middle East. Actually, he was mad before the winter started and he looked it. Unkind people likened him to a petrol pump or a visitor from Mars. He was very short, had an enormous bald head and looked something like a hairless peach on matchsticks. Above all he was a racing fanatic and when I first met him his wife had just left him after he'd told her, in a moment of intoxication and great frankness, that in his considered opinion the great Italian racehorse, Ribot, was far more important than she was. Anyway, there he was living alone in an enormous flat opposite Battersea Park when the snow began to fall. Disaster. All racing cancelled.

For days on end we fidgeted in the pub reliving the glories of our past wins and near misses nigh desperate for a horse to bet on. Then, in our third week of the great cold spell, Caspar walked into the pub one day and said, 'D'you fancy coming racing tonight?' I pointed out that there wasn't any racing except in Australia and California but he said, 'Yes there is. At my place tonight at seven o'clock.' I asked him what sort of racing. Was it some daft kid's game or card game?

'No,' he said, his eyes shining brightly, 'it's cat racing.' Of course, I knew he was bonkers, but having nothing better to do I duly popped round to his flat at the appointed hour.

Now Caspar had two cats and having been something of a socialist in his early days they went by the names of Keir Hardie and George Lansbury. Keir Hardie was a vicious, black bastard of an animal and Lansbury was a rather neurotic marmalade. When I got to the flat, was led into the kitchen and had the plan explained to me, I knew for certain that Caspar had gone beyond recall. He'd actually laid out a racecourse along the passage from the kitchen to the front door — a good forty feet. And this is what he told me in all seriousness.

'Normally, of course, I'd have arranged a flat race but since we're in the middle of the National Hunt season I've built a hurdle course. There are four flights of hurdles,' and he showed me four sticks at equal intervals along the passage that had dish cloths draped over them, 'and I haven't fed the cats for two days. Now I'm going to place a saucer of tinned salmon by the front door, give them a sniff of it, bring them back to the kitchen and then let them go.'

Well, I was fascinated by cats and man and although I thought he'd gone a bit far in not feeding the wretched things for two days I couldn't resist having half a crown with him on Lansbury at 3-1. At those odds he seemed like good value. We stood in the kitchen and had a drink and, being something of a meticulous stickler as well as lunatic, he actually made me wait until 7.30 p.m. That, he said, was the time of the race. The clock ticked round and we squatted on the floor holding an animal each and then they were 'off'.

Keir Hardie never attempted to jump. He crashed through every hurdle in his desperation to get to the tinned salmon and never once did he appear to be in any danger of falling. George Lansbury was a great disappointment to me. He hit the top of every jump and was beaten by an easy three lengths. Although I realised that any responsible body of medical men, let alone the RSPCA, would have had us committed if they'd witnessed the scene, I have to admit I was hooked. While Hardie and Lansbury attacked the salmon Caspar and I retired to the sitting room, hereinafter referred to as the Steward's Room, to discuss the next meeting and we arranged it for the following weekend.

Came the Saturday and Caspar had gone even further round the bend. He'd invited the copywriter called Tom who'd brought a tabby with him all the way from Wimbledon and if you know anything about racing you'll know that they don't travel all that way for the fresh air. The tabby was called Samantha — Caspar kept referring to her as a 'filly' — and she had extremely powerful-looking quarters. If she could jump, I thought, she might be a good thing. It was then that Caspar asked Tom and me for a pound each.

'What the hell for?' I asked him.

'Well, all races are run for prize money and owners have to put up the entrance money, don't they?' I agreed to that and then asked him what we were racing for.

'The winner,' said Caspar, 'gets a bottle of Sauterne and the second gets twenty Players.'

When we lined them up in the kitchen doorway you could see the poor blighters had been on a diet alright and Kier Hardie was dribbling, he was so hungry. It was more or less the same story all over again. Hardie was never going to be much in the way of a jumper but he was a real speed merchant. He won again, this time by about two lengths, and we reckoned that Samantha and George Lansbury just about dead heated for second place. While they tore into the salmon we had a bit of a conference in the Steward's Room. 'It's going to be a bit boring if Keir Hardie keeps on winning all the time,' I ventured. Caspar nodded in agreement and then a madder than usual look came into his eyes.

'I've got it,' he said and I have to admit that he then came out with the greatest brainwave since the invention of whisky.

'We'll handicap them.'

'And how in the hell d'you propose to do that?' I asked.

'With the kitchen scale weights,' he answered and I knew I was in the presence of genius.

We couldn't wait until the next weekend so Caspar and Tom put their cats on an immediate crash course diet and we met two nights later. We agreed that if horses get three pounds for a length then cats should get an ounce for a length. Caspar pulled the kitchen scales out of a cupboard — about the only thing his wife had left him — and he then proceeded to fix a three ounce weight with the aid of some Sellotape on to Keir Hardie's back. He didn't like it and I didn't care much for the dodgy look in Tom's eye as we got them ready for the Off. Samantha was very much on edge and a few years in the racing game have made me easily suspicious. I was even more so when Tom asked us — dead nonchalantly — if either Caspar or I would like to lay him four fivers on her. We declined and I had a quid at threes on Lansbury, who I was convinced was improving with every race.

At eight o'clock they got off to a level if rather loud start. For once Keir Hardie was never in the hunt. Lansbury raised my hopes momentarily at the halfway stage but Samantha won from trap to line. She did more than that. She jumped the saucer of salmon and tried to crash out of the flat through the letter box. You'd have thought Caspar was Lord Derby the way he carried on. He actually pulled a red handkerchief out of his pocket, which I correctly guessed to be cat racing's equivalent of the red flag at the races, denoting a Steward's Enquiry, and we retired to the Steward's Room to debate the debacle. I tumbled what had happened right away. I know bloody writers, even copywriters.

'You doped your cat, didn't you, Tom?' I said, opening his prize of a bottle of Mouton Cadet. 'What *are* you talking about?' he said.

'Come on, you gave it a Dexedrine or some sort of pep pill, didn't you?' Of course, he denied it, but I knew I was right. I also knew, as the evening wore on and as we drank more and more, that my cat racing days were over. Caspar was very nearly due for a strait-jacket. He got completely carried away. Very pompously he put down his empty glass at the end of the evening and turned to Tom and told him, 'I'm sorry to have to tell you, Tom, that I agree with Jeffrey and I have no alternative but to inform you that you are "warned off".'

The words echoed in my head as I sat on the tube going home. The phrase so dreaded by those had up in front of the Jockey Club and now I'd heard it in all seriousness in a Battersea flat. Warned off. Good God, I thought, Caspar really is mad. As I got home, I noticed it was beginning to thaw. What, I wondered, would Caspar do now with Keir Hardie and George Lansbury? Turn them out in a field for the summer, I shouldn't be surprised. Nothing was beyond him. And thereby hangs a sequel.

A few months later — you're not going to believe this but I swear it's true — Caspar moved to St John's Wood and I bumped into him one morning on Primrose Hill as I was returning home from an all-night party. He was standing on top of the hill itself, looking, would you believe, at something through a pair of binoculars.

'What the hell are you doing?' I asked him.

'Cantering Keir Hardie,' he told me. I insinuated that he must be joking but he merely said, 'We could be in for a very dry summer. A drought, in fact. In that case, what with hard going, the fields could cut up. Not many trainers would want to risk horses on that sort of ground.'

To date, Caspar hasn't actually been carried off to the funny farm. I see him from time to time and I'm told he now earns a living writing pornography since he got the sack from his embassy for spending too much time in the betting shop. Mind you, if it ever does come to it again and we do have to race cats this winter I think it might be much better if we did it with an electric mouse.

11. IN THE DEFENCE OF GOSSIP AND OTHER MEDIA AFFAIRS: *Taki*

IN DEFENCE OF GOSSIP

Sainte-Beuve called the duc de Saint-Simon '*l'espion du siècle*' ('the spy of the century'), and, thank God, the duc was. Were it not for Saint-Simon's chronicles of life at Versailles, a great majority of us would probably adhere to a Sam Goldwyn version of what went on in the rarefied and ritualised society of the Sun King.

In the eighteenth century, when the duc wrote his *Mémoires* of life under Louis XIV and Louis XV, he was considered a terrible gossip. Well, perhaps one day Liz Smith or Herb Caen may be called the Saint-Simon of our time, although I doubt it. Neither of them dwells on the kind of telling detail that Saint-Simon used in order to describe society, nor is either likely to be as subtly bitchy as he was. Their trouble, simply put, is that they are too kind.

On the other hand, no one has ever accused Nigel Dempster — England's greatest gossip writer — of being nice. He believes that four hundred years from now, people will read him to find out what twentieth-century life was really like. He explains his keyhole type of journalism this way: 'I look at people's sex lives, especially those of prominent people, because the personal habits that manifest themselves only when observed close up are the ones that lead to detection of flaws that might influence public performance.' Dempster is no hatchet man. He may be tough, but he is fair. Yes, he scrutinises the sex lives of Prince Charles and of the girls Charles goes out with. But before him, everything one read

138

about the royal family was like the stuff Madison Avenue puts out for its best clients.

But to get back to Saint-Simon. Ah, but he was a diarist, a chronicler, people say in order to elevate him above modern gossip writers. Well, I say that Saint-Simon's eye for detail was as sharp as his nose for scandal, and he wrote some of the best gossip of all time. How else would we know that all gentlemen grew the nails of their little fingers or carried pocket combs so that a scratch at the door could tell the lady within that it was time for an assignation? (One never knocked at Versailles.)

When I read history, I always find that it's the gossip that gives the flavour — and often, the substance — of who people were and what life was like.

Without gossip, history comes out flat, dull, and far removed from its original purpose. Public accomplishments are simply not enough. If they were, we'd have passport-like descriptions of the various characters in history, and *c'est tout*.

Diaries and other subjective records are the concentrated essence of history. Only by reading Talleyrand's memoirs, for instance, can one begin to understand the amorality of his political ambitions — and his reputation for immorality in general. (Although I am not sure that it is immoral to make love with members of the same family from three generations, as he did with the duchesses de Dino: *grandmère*, *mère*, and *fille*.)

There are two kinds of gossip: the puerile kind, which is time-wasting by half-wits; and the other, which informs and helps to define the age. Homer's songs about the Trojan Wars and Ulysses' wanderings are an example of the latter. They could not have survived without the impulse to pass on a good story. Of course, in those days people gossiped about the bravery of their heroes and how they managed to beat the will of the gods — not about, say, what Warren Beatty and his sister think of Teddy Kennedy and his sisters.

Much of what we know about medieval history is sheer gossip. For instance: King John of England is known to us as Bad King John because of the insane prejudices of a couple of monk chroniclers — for no other reason and certainly with no other proof. Our knowledge of Charlemagne is based on hearsay, as is evident in the Einhard biography of him.

Any history of life in eighteenth-century England would be incomplete without the writings of Horace Walpole, who recorded the most interesting things, by far, that we know about his father, Robert, a prime minister. Walpole was a great friend of Voltaire, who was not only the father of the French Revolution but also the greatest of gossips.

Which brings me back to a certain kind of academic history. It is as dry as dust, and there is nothing the academics hate to admit more than that. But they fail when they neglect the intimate moments of history. Without these glimpses into people's private lives, history is boring as well as intellectually dishonest. The serious argument is this: Can a historian write the life of Frederick the Great, for example, yet ignore Voltaire's letters about him — letters that were full of catty, bitchy, and witty remarks? I say no; as a historian one cannot. As a bore one can.

Malcolm Muggeridge, a serious writer if there ever was one, said that 'who sleeps with whom is intrinsically more interesting than who votes for whom.' Let me explain. If, for example, the British electorate had known in advance that Ted Heath was, at best, totally uninterested in sex, they would have been prepared for the kind of false machismo that Heath later exhibited in his confrontation with the miners — a confrontation that brought him and the Tory party down. Now that we know about Teddy Kennedy's philandering (not a bad thing in itself), it is important to find out whom he has philandered with. Because as we all know, the only way to judge a man nowadays is by the women he goes around with.

Give me a good, gossipy history book, and I forget about women and wine. The examples are infinite — something like Madame de la Tour du Pin's biography of Marie-Antoinette. The lady-in-waiting's writings about the tragic queen's last days make extraordinary reading. Samuel Pepys's diaries are an essential account for the light that they throw on the everyday life and ways of the Stuart court, and they are a delight because of their gossipy style. Ditto William Hickey's writings, as well as those of the Comte de las Cases on the last years of Napoleon. Swift, Defoe — the list is endless. Until today.

Now we have to put up with Christina Crawford's, Britt Ekland's, and even John Dean's self-serving tales. Unfortunately, these people don't help us to understand anything at all. In today's quick-buck culture, publishers can cash in on cheap gossip. They're not interested in history or wit. Nothing like what the gossip tells us about Voltaire on his deathbed: when a priest asked him if he renounced the devil, the great man looked surprised and said that this was no time to make new enemies. Either they don't make them like Voltaire anymore or they don't gossip the way they used to.

ON THE BOX

New York

The David Susskind Show has been the longest-running talk show ever since that catastrophic day when the tube became an integral part of American culture, as well as being the best proof I know that H.L. Mencken got it right when he said that you never went broke underestimating the public's taste. I was on the Susskind show and was immediately convinced that Susskind would never go off the air, or go broke for that matter. He is a silver-haired, smooth-talking Hollywood type with the smile of a politician and the tan that goes with it. After five minutes he convinced me that he had the integrity of a hyena and the knowledge of those bearded types that take Khomeini seriously.

Nevertheless, the Show was a great success. How could it not have been, as the subjects Mr Susskind zeroed in on were Warren Beatty's aptitude in bed, Jackie O's profligacy, and the fact that Barbra Streisand's boyfriend was able to successfully switch from being a hairdresser to a producer. Susskind has the reputation of speaking his mind and, although this particular talent of his limits his conversation, we did manage to rise above his favourite subjects when I mentioned politics. I said that Jerry Brown's face were the only two things I didn't like about him. After a pregnant pause that seemed a lifetime, he finally caught on. And got furious.

After saying something about Europeans not being able to know anything about American politics because of the distance, he returned to safer subjects. Like telling a story about Warren Beatty's capability of discussing a multi-million dollar deal over the phone while in the process of copulating. The Show ran for two hours and I'm afraid that, among the people who don't move their lips when they read, it must have elicited the same kind of admiration one would feel for a streaker at Queen Victoria's funeral.

The depressing fact about television was never more obvious until after the show. Even close friends of mine who have never bothered to read anything I write mentioned the fact that they've seen me on the telly. Which might be indicative of the friends I have as well as of American culture in general. In terms of exerting influence over the minds of a nation, history offers no parallels to the power wielded by the greedy, crude, illiterate men who choose programmes for the television networks. If I had the power I would send all those moral quacks over to Iran in exchange for the hostages, then I would destroy that miserable country knowing fully well I would be doing civilisation a favour.

Which brings up the question of who runs television. Usually the faces the public sees on television are there because they have passed tests administered by the gate-keepers. The tests check the appearances of the prospective television personalities, their sense of humour, eye contact, warmth etc. There is lip service paid to the need for innovation, but very little enthusiasm for different ideas. Nobody ever wants to rock the boat. Talk shows, especially, make sure the presenters are either selling a book or an album or a movie, but never an idea. This format has made Paley rich and famous in America, and will probably make Murdoch, Grade and whoever else gets hold of the television licences in England, just as rich and just as infamous.

IRA AUTHOR

Phony books for fast profits by ghost writers are making good writing redundant and bringing about the greatest change in publishing since Gutenberg's invention. Although the down-marketing of publishing tastes is nothing new — shoddy, superficial books have always sold better than good, serious works — it was nonetheless true that book publishing was a trade that clung to the standards of good writing as passionately as an upper class Englishman clings to his aitches. (Profits from published garbage enabled good writers to appear in print.)

No longer. Good writing is definitely to be avoided at all costs. And due to high-powered salesmanship and marketing techniques, celebrities, jet-setters, movie stars and half-witted aristocrats are now standing shoulder to shoulder with the likes of Shakespeare, Milton, Swift and Waugh.

The breakthrough came about when the function of journalism — where a person researches and writes about those involved in an event — was made redundant by publishers intent on signing up the participant. (What I could have done with Napoleon after Waterloo, sighs Lord Weidenfeld.) Of course most participants today (celebrities) have trouble composing a breakfast list and so ghost writers have suddenly become as valuable a commodity as an ounce of pure Peruvian at a trendy New York party. And the 'beautiful people' are pursued by literary groupies as Hemingway was during his glorious years.

The latest jet-setter to turn writer is Ira von Furstenberg. Her book will be found in gold-blocked cloth, will cost approximately as much as England's defence budget, and is on Beauty. What kind of beauty? Why, the natural one, of course. Beauty like that of Jacqueline de Ribes, Elise Goulandris, Helen Rochas and Gloria Guinness. All around sixty, if not more, with a bank account in excess of fifty million pounds.

Ira is uniquely qualified to write on the subject. Her mother is an Agnelli, she is forty-two years old, has lifted as many parts of her anatomy as a pickpocket lifts wallets during the tourist season, and has attended almost as many parties during the last twenty years. Incidentally, Ira eloped with Prince Hohenlohe when she was fifteen, some years after giving up her higher education. Her brother, Egon, has also become a scribe. He received a fabulous advance to write on Power. Needless to add, the effete Egon is as qualified to discourse about power as Millwall fans are to write about good sportsmanship. Egon, a dress designer, is being published first in America.

Another Furstenberg, this one by marriage, has already become a best selling authoress. Diane, ex-wife of Egon and born Diane Cohen in Belgium, 'wrote' an opus about her beauty secrets. It was very successful and she is at present planning a follow-up. Still one more quintessential jet-setter batting out deathless prose is Charlotte Ford Niarchos. She is better known as Henry's daughter. Charlotte is writing on Success. She is guaranteed good sales, especially in France where she spent long years learning French. They are still talking about her immortal riposte when greeted by a gentleman with 'Bonjour'. 'Daddy's in Detroit' she answered back.

Needless to say, the ultimate jet-setter, Jackie O, has not exactly missed the opportunity to sell her brains. Her book on the Russian style of dress was presumed to be of such extraordinary interest to the reading public that the editors were willing to let fourteen other writers starve to death.

Although books on health and fashion predominate among celebrity authors, politics are a close third, after sports. It is a well-known fact that John Dean's Watergate revelations became a best seller because of Taylor Branch's ghost job. Branch got little for his troubles. He plans, however, to come to England and drive a better deal. This one with, guess who, Lord Weidenfeld.

BIG MONEY

Recently, I was sitting in the smallest room of my house — that particular place where H.G. Wells liked to read what the critics had to say about his books — when I was interrupted by the ring of the telephone. I immediately recognised the heavily

accented mid-Atlantic twang of Miss Christina Onassis. She
was calling from St Moritz and was furious. It seems that one
of her ex-husbands had seen me on television and had heard
me call her, his ex-wife, a vegetable. 'How dare you call me
that,' she hissed over the transatlantic cable. I tried desperately to recollect what I had said that was causing so much
concern.

It was during a Saturday night television programme in
which I made an appearance. Russell Harty asked me if it
was true that I had turned down a large amount of money from
an American publisher to write Christina's biography. Harty
had acquired that information from an item of Nigel
Dempster's in the *Daily Mail*. Dempster had written that the
reason I refused the offer was because I considered her to be
a vegetable. I cannot remember exactly what I said but one
thing I'm sure of: the first person to have used the word
vegetable in connection with Christina was not me. I tried to
make fun by telling Christina, whom I have known all my life,
that I love to eat vegetables but would not want to eat her.
She was not amused.

Here is something which angers *me*. The Alexander Onassis
Foundation was formed after Aristotle died in 1975, in memory
of his only son who had died in an aeroplane accident two
years previously. The Foundation is a charitable one, and an
enormous amount of publicity accompanied the announcement of its creation. Five years later, it has just announced
its first international awards. As I flew into Athens I could hear
the porters carrying my luggage complaining about it:
'Couldn't they find anybody a bit more needy?' they said.
This was because with a great fanfare the Foundation had
announced that £100,000 will be awarded to . . . Harold
Macmillan and Simone Weil, the French Lady President of
the European Parliament, that august body in Brussels that is
equalled in ferocity and prestige only by the United Nations.

Now I ask you. Is the old man climbing from his tomb?
Is it possible that such an enormous amount will go to two
people who not only have no need of it, but, as far as I am
concerned, have done very little to deserve it? Unless I am
mistaken, I thought the Foundation was a charitable one.

Macmillan does not need any charity. Ms Weil, too, needs none. She got her award, according to the Foundation, 'for bringing nations closer together', whatever that means. Supermac got his for ecology. Something to do with some statement he made about the Parthenon, I believe. The announcement used high-flown language but made a Freudian slip. It actually stated that the selection committee members were unbiased. I believe the contrary. Soon, that greatest of humbugs, Helen Vlachos, a member of the committee, will receive a *Legion d'Honneur* or something to that effect. It will be a quid pro quo deal. So, Christina, if I've insulted you, I apologise. You are not a vegetable. But the people you'll be addressing this Saturday, two winners excluded, are, and rotten ones at that.

SCANDALISED

My friend Nigel Waymouth is a hard-working and talented artist who specialises in the old-fashioned art of portraiture. He recently had an exhibition of his work and Emma Soames, the gifted daughter of that terribly nice Mugabe man's fat friend, wrote about him and his paintings. Emma is a friend of Waymouth's wife, Lady Victoria, and was obviously trying to be nice. Because of her efforts she only got two things wrong, both minor details. She spelled Waymouth's surname wrong and referred to him as finding time to dab away at still-lifes.

Now I don't mind people misspelling my name and I believe others shouldn't either. But when it comes to words like 'dab' where working is concerned I become a raging ayatollah, full of hate. Waymouth takes his work very seriously and spends endless hours going over minute details. Unlike some of those modern art phonies who splash away at a canvas and expect you to see the esoteric meaning of it all, Nigel actually paints the human form and makes it look exactly the way a human body does look. So 'dab' was an unfortunately verb to use because it might have suggested to her dilettante readers that the artist, too, was like them. So Emma gets a nine for effort and a four for execution.

If I give the impression that I am being a bit hard on my buddy Emma it is because I am off hacks in general and gossip writers in particular. Nor am I too happy with the Soames family. Just as I was arriving in a civilised country after my trials and tribulations in the birthplace of demagogy, my heart beat a little faster when I saw Mrs Thatcher and the rest of the Cabinet waiting. I presumed they were there to congratulate me on surviving three weeks and one attempt on my life in Greece but, alas, they were there to hug and kiss Emma's father for his Houdini-like act in extricating the UK from its dodgiest predicament since Dunkirk.

But to get back to the gossip mongers. Ever since the *News of the World* said that a certain nubile lady was immune to my charm, and that I was in turn interested in her because her father would one day assume a different name, I have been the laughing stock of London. Even Nando, the walking death machine who is Annabel's doorman, was disgusted. In order to let me in the other night he forced me to break a brick with my fist (along with one of my knuckles) just to prove to him that I was still a man and not a social-climbing mouse.

I don't know why all the gossip columnists suddenly find it funny to make fun of a poor little Greek boy trying to make his way through English society; if at least they got it right I wouldn't mind as much. One Lady gossip had me going out with Lady Falkender. She quickly retracted when Marcia threatened to sue her as she has never in her life ever gone out either with a fascist like me nor a man worth less than 300 million pounds, an amount I hope to have by next year but do not have at present.

But the coup de grâce of bad taste was delivered by, who else, the doyen of scandal, Nigel Dempster himself. He wrote that I had a long name and that I was out to marry a member of the British aristocracy. Nothing could be further from the truth. And as usual he got all his facts wrong. Not by any stretch of the imagination could my name be considered long, there are only four letters for God's sake. I certainly do not want to marry a member of the British aristocracy because I am not a necrophiliac and do not plan to turn into one in the near future. Furthermore, I consider the Taki family far superior to the barbarians who were still climbing trees and wearing furs while my ancestor was building the Parthenon.

Taki I was the brother of Alexander the Great's niece. He fought with Alexander against the Persians and was given great lands in that miserable country now known as Iran. He left almost immediately when he encountered the first Iranians and the Taki family afterwards surfaced as consuls in the Roman senate. The last great Taki fought alongside Constantine Paleologos in Constantinople when the infamous Mohammed stormed the city in 1453. The emperor died but Taki survived. His descendant was one of the Czar's prime ministers during the early 18th century and then the family eventually returned to Greece to fight and gain the country's liberation from the Turks (probably the first mistake ever by the Taki dynasty).

So how could anyone be as dumb or naive as to think that I need to mix with those funny people one sees standing next to horses, smiling like half-wits and always red-faced. The last thing Dempster got very wrong, and he will be sued by my father for it, was when he said the family was worth only £200 million. Poor fool. It's more, much more.

12. GREAT MEDIA BORES OF ENGLAND: *Jeffrey Bernard*

IN DEPTH

Get this: 'Charlotte Rampling's eyes for instance; those twin orbs of ineffable other-worldliness in whose depth cinema audiences have floundered exquisitely for a decade are, in the daylight privacy of her own home, the precise colour of a turned-off television screen.' It's marvellous isn't it?

That was a soupçon of an *Observer* interview with Charlotte Rampling and Jean Michael Jarre written by Sally Vincent. I must say when Buchwald goes, when the Perelman pen runs dry, and if Coren retires, then there is always Vincent to snap us out of taking life too seriously. Whatever made anyone on the *Observer* think that Charlotte Rampling was of any interest whatsoever is something of a mystery. But then the qualification necessary to be written about on the Women's Page is solely to be female. I'd better own up though. Not only have I received no money for jam recently, I'm absolutely choked about the fact that I shall never ever be interviewed by a 'real writer' from a posh newspaper, and I'd like to be because I'm very silly and very vain. If only I could be the tool whereby some hack could hope to find immortality on the pages of a newspaper then I think it might go like this.

'Jeffrey Bernard's eyes, twin pools of tired anger and bitterness, flicker with the pathetic expectancy of a man searching a newly vacated sofa for mislaid currency. His hair is precisely the colour of manmade ice and his teeth have the brittle falseness of a society hostess's welcome. When I called on him and his wife, Marie Zso-Zso Labore, in their

Montparnasse apartment I was struck almost immediately by
an odour of musty sweetness which seemed strangly out of
place in a room literally heaped with Henri Onze furniture.

'With an unfinished autobiography and unstarted novel
behind him, to say nothing of two accepted but unperformed
plays, it was strangely moving to me that he should be whist-
ling the Stamitz Symphonia Concertante in D major while
his wife contended herself with provençale thoroughness in
making the salad dressing. I asked about the odd smell and
Marie, waif-like in her simplicity, glanced at her husband and
told me, "Oh that, that's the odour of self-pity".

'She dresses unobtrusively in old curtains but he clings
defiantly to grey flannels — a symptom and reminder of his
pebble-dashed past. Conversationally they are on an odd
frequency, the hi-fidelity of the incoherent, and yet what they
say crashes into one's mind with all the abrasiveness of acid
biting into copperplate. For example, I asked him what he
was working on at the moment. "Well, basically, and I'm
simply using words as thought-transfers now, I'm not actually
doing anything in so far as you could call doing something
anything." At that moment, encapsulated for me by the poig-
nancy of his almost unwilling smile, Marie looked up and
said, "Yes, basically, that is it."

'They asked me to stay for lunch. Marie served us some
superb pain grillé which she passed around on the willow-
pattern plate that she insisted they took with them to Paris
when Jeffrey's world crashed ten years ago in London.
"Actually," she told me, "it's the last tangible connection
we have with the old days in Camden Passage."

'He groaned and poured himself another cognac. Suddenly
I was aware that Marie and Jeffrey were relating in terrify-
ingly stark but nevertheless intimate and self-explanatory
sentences that were the coded chips of their marriage. "Yes,"
he said. Just that, no more. She looked at him and whispered,
"Of course. This is it." Then he walked over to the record
player and put on the Rasumowski No 2. It seemed the right
time for me to leave. Goodbye was understood, not said.
How does anyone say goodbye to a recurring dream? It would
have been pretentious.'

BLOCK BUSTING

I have recently had a sneak preview of two monstrously
long and tedious novels. They weren't sent to me for review,
they were given to me by a disenchanted reviewer. One of
them is the new John Masters epic saga called *Now, God be
Thanked* and the other is by Philip Rock and called *The
Passing Bells*. The Masters effort doesn't peter out until page
589 whereas the Rock book is a mere sprinter lasting only
464 pages. I am beginning to get the hang of what's required
to persuade publishers that there's a bestseller on the drawing
board and a fairly intellectually limited public that they're
reading the literary real McCoy. Galsworthy lives.

If he doesn't, pretty mediocre reincarnations of him do.
Length is good. Fat books are good. Although Galsworthy
springs to mind it is, in fact, more of a modern American
trend and maybe today's formula for the saga got started with
Dreiser's *An American Tragedy*. It needs a writer who's
totally devoted to himself — fancy wanting to write 589 pages
— and who, like Deighton or Forsythe, thinks he is pretty
bloody good. How else could you think what you've got to say
needs a pulped equatorial rainforest to put it in? Anyway,
the recipe for the epic-saga is quite simple really and just
needs a lot of time and typewriting.

First, take a family, preferably an upper middle-class one,
and follow it for no less than three generations. Then take
the servants from downstairs, include their pathetic loves,
dreams and hopes, and fold them carefully into the rest of the
mixture. Put this into an epically nostalgic period and then
stew very slowly and gently for 500 to 600 pages at IQ mark 65.

For this recipe you need a family that will remind today's
readers that our values have gone to pot and that life was
sweeter between 1900 and 1945. Lord Haslemere and his
wife live sumptuously but quietly on a large estate in Sussex.
The war clouds are gathering over Europe while they dig into
the Old English breakfast marmalade and devilled kidneys,
and they know things will never be quite the same again. They
have four children, Tom, Dick, Jane and Sarah. Tom is at
Oxford, has fair hair, is brilliant, gentle and about to row as

stroke in the Boat Race while Dick is dark, surly, randy and a rotter. The girls are of the same mould. Jane helps the local poor, likes Mozart, loves Fred the gardener's lad and will become a nurse on the Somme while Sarah gets laid something rotten in London by Dick's best friend.

Just to show that all of us go through the mill we have to add some flavouring in the form of the odd flashback where, lo and behold, it turns out that Lord and Lady Haslemere too have had something other between their legs than a hunter in bye-gone days. Expert chefs like John Masters, by the way, simply love the idea of the upper classes being as randy as us gamekeepers, butlers, batmen and bohemians. Where the strongest essence of fiction is added is in the effort to show us that Haslemere and his ilk are just as capable as hoi polloi of unhappiness and sensitivity. This is shown by having Tom write verse, Jane joining the suffragette movement, Dick winning a posthumous V.C. and Sarah dying in childbirth in a Cumberland croft. All this is watched with a patronising fidelity by cook, Heathers, Nancy the housemaid — a flighty girl prone to allowing the master to have his way — and Wilson the gamekeeper who has a special understanding with Haslemere.

The good children make out while Dick and Sarah snuff it and Haslemere is left gazing at the dying embers in the hearth of the library fire. It is almost as though he can hear the echoes from the past of, first the Afghan bullets whining past his ear and then the church bells ringing in Midhurst the day he got married and then again on Armistice Day. Lady Haslemere looks up, knows exactly what's going on through the old warrior's head and she takes his hand as they go up the 40 stairs to Bedfordshire. 'It *was* worth it, wasn't it darling?' he says as she turns out the light and as a fox barks in the distance. 'Of course it was, my dear.'

Well, I suppose it was if the publisher's advance was big enough.

FOURTH CHANNEL

Prepare now to be disappointed. When the new television channel begins transmissions and makes several businessmen millionaires overnight, you may not get quite the programmes you were hoping for. Several media whizz kids have told me that it's going to be a wow and all because of the enormous amount of talent, vision, genius and artistic sensibility owned by a few in this country and simply screaming to be let loose on a deserving public. There will be a little something for everybody, from the humblest of *Coronation Street* addicts to those who prefer their quartets to be late. Some of it might just ring a bell.

8.00 *Morning Service*. Recorded at St Paul's Cathedral in August 1979, on the occasion of the Thanksgiving Service for Lord Boothby's recovery from a broken leg.

9.00 *News*. With Helen Mirren. Weather.

9.10 *Home Today*. A magazine programme for Women. Sally Vincent talks to some very dull people who aren't having affairs. Jill Tweedie demonstrates how to perform a bilateral testesectomy. Irma Kurtz talks to some women about their problem of liking men. Bel Mooney talks to a woman who sailed singlehanded across the Ruislip Lido and Fergus Cashin explains the workings of Teetotallers Anonymous.

10.00 *Un Peu de l'Autre*. Starring Jeanne Moreau and Peter Barkworth. The story of a middle-aged man's pathetic, sad and sometimes hilarious quest for a bit on the side. Produced by Ken Trodd. Directed by Joe McGrath. (Made in sepia.) With Polish subtitles.

12.00 *Sports Forum*. Silent recording of the fight between James J. Corbett and Bob Fitzsimmons with an inter-round talk by Christopher Booker on 'The Meaning of Aggression'. Plus pro-celebrity backgammon. This week Nick the Greek *v*. Denis Norden. Also, beagling from Chatsworth and cock-fighting from Epping Forest.

12.30 *Man to Man*. David Dimbleby talks to seven 'Men of the World'. 1: Frederic Raphael. 'Life is incredibly sad.' So says Frederic Raphael the novelist, poet, scriptwriter and *homme de nos jours*. He explains some of the agonies of success and shatters the myth that money, fame and charm bring happiness. Acutely sensitive, Raphael fled to the Dordogne ten years ago where he is now taken seriously by his family and local *charcuterie*. At his Suffolk home he talks about the unimportance of money.

1.00 *News*. With Ivy Compton-Burnett. Weather.

1.10 *What Next?* An afternoon entertainment for the self-employed. Bernard Levin describes his recent holiday in Siberia. Yehudi Menuhin shows you how to make yoghurt. Stella Richman talks about the difficulties she encountered in making her 30-part series of *The Cloister and the Hearth*. Diana Quick explains how to write a novel and Frank Muir explains how to get an advance on it. John Betjeman visits Bethnal Green tube station.

3.30 *Field and Feather*. Did you know that the average vole weighs 1⅓ oz? David Attenborough has spent 15 years filming a day in the life of a vole near Ipswich where inhabitants are fighting to save this creature from Japanese factory lorries.

4.25 *Afternoon Drama*. Cry For Help. Starring Peter Barkworth, George Cole, Gwen Watford. The Story of two middle-aged men's pathetic, sad and sometimes hilarious pursuit of a bit of spare.

5.30 *Pun My Soul*. A literary parlour game pontificated over by Robert Robinson. Angela Rippon reads the Fifth Decade of Cantos by Ezra Pound and Keith Waterhouse shows his collection of cigarette cards and other momentos from a deprived childhood. Alan Brien sets the quiz, 'When Did I Say That?'

7.00 *News*. With Edna O'Brien. Weather.

10.45 *One For The Road*. Presented live from pubs round about Britain.

11.45 *And So To Bed*. Late Night Movie. Starring Peter Barkworth and Capucine in a story of middle-aged man's pathetic, futile and sometimes hilarious attempt to leave his wife, with tragic consequences. Brilliant cameo by John Hurt as Gerald Hamilton.

3.00am *Closedown*. With Vita Sackville-West and Academy of St Martin's-in-the-Fields. Bach and Berg.

MUG'S DIARY

Lunched with Betty and the Pinters. Talk revolved around the Social Democrats and the stupidity of carnal lust. Harold and I agreed that Foot is something of an ignoble fellow but we fell out over the symbolism of Long John Silver having only one leg. Betty said that it was Stevenson's repressed castration wish. This I can't believe. Antonia said she wrote down everything she read from Buchan and Carlyle in long hand before she later dictated it to her blind German secretary. Jenkins, it seems, never really wanted to join the Common Market in the first place. That evening we walked across Hyde Park to the Gulbenkians. I told Asif that had Margaret Thatcher wished to have joined the Labour Party she could have become another Nye Bevan. The crocuses are doing splendidly.

18 March 1981. Met Bernard Levin in Fortnums for tea. He told me a little about Richard Wagner whom, it seems, he knew pretty well. Apparently the old Hun once bounced Bernard on his knee in Gstaad. At all events the memory lingers for Levin who, I can't help thinking, could have made much more of himself if he wasn't inclined to ridiculous infatuations. After leaving him I wandered into Hatchards and saw Tolstoy's latest novel. Quite frankly I feel he needs a tremendous amount of cutting but there's no denying his innate talent. He seems to have a tremendous grasp of the reality of life in real terms but, here again, I think there's a man who is endangered by his stupid fascination with carnal pleasure. Of course, he likes to call it love, but we know it's pure lust on the Lloyd George scale. Late home to Betty. Camomile tea and to bed with Randolph's memoirs. Tatty stuff.

21 March 1981. Considered suicide again for the umpteenth time this year but rejected it. How long can I put it off? The quality of life is becoming more tawdry every day. At lunchtime I met Denis Healey in Whites. Superb oysters and lobster Newburg. Denis seemed rather jaded and pessimistic about Foot finding him a decent post in the next Government. God only knows what makes him think there will be a next

Government. He surprised me somewhat by saying that he was bullied at school and joined the Communist Party at the time I was spying in Cairo for M18. Basically, he seems a good man, but I can't help feeling that his delight in good food and wine will ultimately destroy him. He reminded me of the time Lord Castlerosse said to me, 'Show me what a man eats and I'll show you what he believes in.' How very true. Walked to Harrods after tea to meet Betty. She looked a little peeky. Must take her to Leningrad for a few days to cheer her up.

22 March 1981. Marvellous to be back in the country after such a boring week in London. Larks ascending, Alpen, skimmed milk, raisins and a sermon from Toby Wilberforce that was one of his better ones. He really has grasped at last the futility of lust but a pity really that he didn't before his wife bore him 14 children. His wife reminded me of an extraordinary woman I met in the Hindu Kush in 1938 when I was there meditating on behalf of Beaverbrook who had suddenly got cold feet about the impending struggle. This old woman — she reminded me tremendously of Rebecca West — had borne 14 children in so many months. Raj Banerjee Mukarjee, the local resident councillor and M17 agent as it turned out later, told me that she had acquired perfect transcendental bliss by the amazing gift of swapping her genitals for her head. She had, as it were, conquered the boredom of lust and could have children by a miraculous thought process. It was rumoured at one time that she was having an affair with Graham Greene but I find that pretty hard to believe. She never struck me as being quite louche enough for dear old Graham.

23 March 1981. Dined with Ronald Biggs, Lord Goodman, Runcible and a delightful but rather dangerous looking woman called Jane Fonda. Apparently the man Biggs has been on a long holiday in Brazil. Says he met lots of Graham's friends there but wasn't, I gathered, connected in any way with Graham G's Foreign Office pals. It seems he has an illegitimate daughter. Oh dear, yet another. It does strike me as being quite awful that these people can lecher after it as Lear's fly. Odd seeing Goodman again who I remember as being a rather endearing little fag I once trashed at St Barts.

The Social Democrats seem to be swelling their ranks and, as I told Shirley Williams that morning, the whole business reminds me horribly of what Hitler told me at Berchtesgaden in October 1938. 'Mark my words Malcolm,' he said, 'give a party a bad name and it's already got three feet on the ladder.' How right he was proved to be. Oddly enough, Betty has still got a sprig of Alpenstock that she picked that day in the garden while Graham and I chatted to the Fuhrer. One thing that struck me profoundly about Herr Hitler was his non-married status and the fact that he was a dedicated vegetarian. I think the Church might have saved Germany from the Nazis had She stood up. Thinking back on those days I sometimes wonder if it wasn't lust and not the bombing that beat the Third Reich. Graham thinks it was both.

SPONGERS

When Taki wrote about how disgusted he was that the Alexander Onassis Foundation had awarded $100,000 to Harold Macmillan and Simone Weil, the French lady president of the European Parliament, and that he wondered why they couldn't have found anyone a little more needy, I was reminded of a letter that appeared in *The Times* about ten weeks ago. It was signed by five or six writers, including Drabble and Wesker I seem to remember, and it was a whine about Arts Council economy cuts. The poor scribes were desperately worried that their foreign jaunts — lecture tours they're called — were going to be knocked on the head and that various third world natives would therefore suffer if they weren't taught the gospel according to the Bodley Head, Heinemann or whoever. Somewhere, the letter implied, a hut-dwelling, blowpipe-hunting cannibal might have to stagger spiritually starved through life because he'd never been told about the works of M. Bragg or seen *Chicken Soup with Barley*. Poor sod.

All this, in turn, reminded me of the remarkable beginnings of that lovely Spaniard, Isaac Albeniz, who survived 14 winters of the greatest severity without a handout from the likes of the Arts Council or a complaining letter to his local rag. Read what *The Oxford Companion to Music* has to say about his early days: 'He appeared as pianist at the age of four, and three years later applied for admission to the Conservatory of Paris, being, however, refused on the grounds of youth. He then studied at the Conservatory of Madrid. At nine he ran away, gave recitals all over Spain, and then hid himself on a vessel for Puerto Rico, giving performances to pay for his passage. Quite alone he undertook a recital tour which extended from Cuba in the east to San Francisco in the west. He came back to Europe at 13, played in Liverpool and London, and studied for a year at Leipzig. He returned penniless to Spain . . .'

Then, and only then, did he get his first handout. Not bad for a little lad who never even knew Charles Osborne or who never appeared on the Russell Harty Show. It makes me wonder how *The Oxford Companion to English Literature* might describe the composite writer 50 years from now.

'Arnold Wobble was born in Somerset in 1942. Educated at a local preparatory school he won a scholarship to Cambridge where, at the age of 19, he underwent an unsuccessful operation to have a silver spoon removed from his mouth. This was later to be the theme of his first six novels — man's failure to alleviate the sufferings of his fellow men. After Cambridge, he went to London where, at a cocktail party at *Encounter*, he met Stephen Spender who lent him £20 to telephone the Arts Council. The Council were deeply impressed by his "demi-sonnets" — he claimed always to be far too busy to write an entire sonnet — and they gave him a grant so that he could take time off to write his first major work, *Apples of my Eye*, a novel about his early days when he worked in a Somerset cider factory. In 1966 he undertook a lecture tour of Chad.

'By now, *Apples of my Eye* was the world's best seller and the Arts Council and Gulbenkian Foundation gave him a further £50,000 to undertake a lecture tour of Heligoland where he was filmed by Humphrey Burton reading *Don Juan* to an audience of lighthouse keepers. Returning to England he was awarded the Christopher Booker prize for 'Services to Humanity' plus £85,000 to enable him to write the first of his one-scene plays for the National Theatre. By now he was the leading light of a group, formed with Melvyn Bragg, known in literary circles as The Country Cousins. In 1979, Norman St John-Stevas awarded him a grant of £500,000 a year so that he could write the life of Martin Amis. He undertook this mammoth task at Blenheim Place, thanks entirely to the National Trust. He died of sunstroke in 1992 while on a lecture tour of Gabon.'

Which reminds me. Would any reader be good enough to sponsor me for an Arts Council grant? You see, I've got this fantastic idea for a play which is all about this fantastic chap who . . . Well, I don't want to give the plot away, but it could be really fantastic.

SENSITIVE

You will probably be saddened to hear that the interview with me conducted by Simon Swank for *Speaking Volumes* and due to have gone out on Dorset Television has been temporarily postponed. So as not to disappoint too many of you I have decided to publish an extract from the transcript.

S.S. 'Most viewers will surely be familiar with what must be your most successful book, *The Cast-Iron Window Box*. Can I ask you what actually made you write such an extraordinary novel?'

J.B. 'Yes. Well, basically, what I wanted to do was to convey to the reader some of the incredible feelings I experienced on my recent travels.'

S.S. 'You travel a lot, do you?'

J.B. 'Yes, you could say that. The particular journey I based *Cast-Iron Window Box* on was one I took from Notting Hill Gate to Queensway. There was this fantastic man sitting opposite me wearing a raincoat and a cap and he suddenly made me feel utterly bewildered and strangely saddened by what had gone before.'

S.S. 'You mean the past or, at least, your past life?'

J.B. 'No. Holland Park.'

S.S. 'I'd like, if I may, to bring up the question of the forceful opening passage of that book which shocked so many critics.

"Once upon a time, etc." What made you choose such a bizarre beginning?'

J.B. 'Yes. I'm glad you asked that. So many people have misunderstood that sentence. I wanted to convey to the reader that I was talking about a singular event in time that had taken place in the past and so evoked what you might call a dreamlike quality, sufficiently sad yet quite horrific in a detached way, and a bit reminiscent of those infantile breakdowns we all knew so well.'

S.S. 'Which brings us to Proust.'

J.B. 'Quite.'

S.S. 'Apart from Proust, who would you say you had been most moved by?'

J.B. 'Well, Pound certainly. A lot of the very early Chatterton — the incredible letters he wrote to his mother from school and, to a certain extent, Captain W.E. Johns.'

S.S. 'What particularly is it about Johns that made you change direction?'

J.B. 'Oh, very much. I think, the passage where Biggles shoots down Von Shtumm in an attempt to tell Algy he is, in fact, homosexual.'

S.S. 'Yes. Can we talk now about sex?'

J.B. 'Yes.'

S.S. 'Critics have said that you're inordinately fond of sex. Would you go along with that?'

J.B. 'Well, only in an erotic sort of way, if you see what I mean. I try to think of sex in purely sexual terms without making moral judgments about what people ought not to do. Of course, in the same way that I use words purely as symbols and not language I use sex intrinsically for sexual contact. It is, after all, an extraordinary way to say "Hallo" to another human being.'

S.S. 'Yes, you made that point quite brilliantly in *Coming and Going*. Can I move on to what you're working on at the moment?'

J.B. 'Yes. Actually it's basically an allegorical paradox. I've drawn a lot on early Donne, late H.E. Bates and the middle period of 'Sapper' that involves Jim Maitland. You could say it's about a man who gets drunk all the time and who doesn't discover himself as he really is until he commits suicide. Of course, he hasn't really committed suicide. It's just closing time.'

S.S. 'You've never written any poetry. Why?'

J.B. 'There's no money in it. Basically, money doesn't matter to me. If I'm writing, then I'm happy. Usually I write for five minutes every Saturday — in longhand or straight onto a secretary — and the rest of the socialising, the literary lunches, the book-signings and free trips are pure grist. I suppose I'm really just using people. I don't actually need money as such except for spending.'

S.S. 'Jeffrey Bernard. Thank you very much.'

J.B. 'Thank *you*.' (Smiles knowingly. Music over — Vivaldi's 'Snowstorm'. Montage sequence — portraits of Byron, Tolstoy, Austen, Dickens and Bernard Levin. Fade out.)

13.   AGAINST THE GRAIN: HIGH LIFE HEROES: *Taki*

A MAN OF PARTS

The best way to describe John Aspinall, inordinate animal lover, extremist campaigner for wildlife preservation, owner of two of the largest private zoos in the world, author, former dandy, political extremist, and gambler extraordinaire, is to use Oscar Wilde's celebrated remark about himself: 'I've put my genius into my life; I've only put my talent into my works.'

Although his sexual preferences are different, Aspinall resembles Wilde in more ways than one. He is a large, imposing man with a wide mouth, blond hair, and very blue eyes. A brilliant raconteur, he has been known to have a hypnotic effect on his audience — even when he addresses groups of miners and preaches the evils of socialism to them. Always conscious of the effect he is creating, Aspinall loves to make outrageous statements. He is the most articulate of men and, naturally, the poorest of listeners.

Born fifty-three years ago in what is now part of Pakistan, Aspinall was a typical product of the British upper middle class during the period of the raj. At age seven, he was shipped back to England to be educated.

During holidays, he lived on a farm and came into contact for the first time with what was to mark him forever: 'the ritualised destruction of harmless and often beautiful species of bird and mammal'. Aspers, as friends call him, calls it a weird, half-baked leftover of our primitive hunting impulse. It has led our governing classes and their imitators, he says, into a cold spiritual void.

After attending the exclusive Rugby School, Aspers did three years of Royal Marines service and then went up to Oxford. It was there that he developed the personality that has been called, among other less flattering things, an elaborate artifice deliberately fashioned to yield anecdotes. He swaggered around the campus sporting a magenta suit, a pink shirt, carrying a cane on one arm and an edition of *Les Fleurs du Mal* under the other. He wrote poetry and he gambled. And he began a lifelong association and friendship with Ian Maxwell-Scott.

Maxwell-Scott can only be described as a rake. A cousin of the Duke of Norfolk, England's premier Catholic duke, Maxwell looks like an absentminded professor, loves wine and gambling, and is the type that laughs at everything he says. Maxwell's love of luxury was never inhibited by the fact that he had gone through his inheritance almost before he got it and that the finer things of life cost money — the one commodity he was consistently incapable of holding on to. He lived in a grand manner, entertained lavishly, and gambled on a scale uncommon even in pre-socialist England when he and Aspers got together, they quickly set standards many Oxford graduates have been unable to match in the years since.

After Oxford, Aspinall came down to London. He and Maxwell-Scott began employing a financial system they thought was infallible. It was called kiting. This consisted of cashing a cheque, then covering it with a second one a day later, followed by a third, and so on. As each cheque took three banking days to clear and was covered by the one issued subsequently, a cash flow developed and was available for gambling. Incidentally, it was immediately after Oxford that Aspers took the deliberate decision never in his life to do any work that he found unpleasant.

Kiting worked for a while until a bad streak of luck brought down the whole system. Maxwell went to the East End of London where many hoboes and down-and-outs hung about. Colonel Robert Aspinall, of the Indian Medical Service, had also returned to England after India's independence. He had John to lunch but refused to bail him out of his various debts.

He did, however, offer £5. And Aspers was not his son. His real father — as Aspinall discovered on his own — was a dashing general of the infantry, General McKilrie Bruce.

Far from being traumatised, Aspers immediately looked up his newly discovered progenitor. But there was no luck there either. As Aspers tells it: 'He seduced my mother under a tamarisk tree on the banks of a stream in Nainital. He was an imposing-looking man, kind but firm. He shook my hand, remembered my mother fondly, and wished me good luck in life. Although he was my real father, he did not give me a fiver.'

In the meantime, his mother had remarried, this time Colonel Sir George Osborne, a kind man who loved Aspers and taught him to love nature. After lying low for a while, Aspers hit an over 300-to-1 shot (as he remembers it) in a horse race. He had procured the money because through his stepfather's connections, he had been offered a job in Nigeria. Instead of paying for his tropical equipment, Aspers put his expense money on a long shot. This was in 1953.

With £7,000 in his pocket, approximately $50,000 by today's standards, Aspers went back to London and began looking for Maxwell-Scott. He found him in a hoboes' hotel, covered with newspapers and reading an old racing sheet. 'Maxwell, we're rich,' he yelled. 'Let's take a suite at the Ritz and start living.' Maxwell's reply was typical: 'The Ritz,' he said, 'has such bad food. Let's try the Connaught.'

Thus the Ritz it was, and that is where Aspers organised poker games. The first floating chemin de fer (chemmy) game began in 1956 in an apartment in Mayfair. Over the next four years, or until gambling became legal in England in 1960 primarily because of his own activities, Aspers organised private games in friends' houses with amazingly profitable results. He participated in the games, covered every bet, and entertained in a manner so lavish that people forgot the amounts being risked.

One of his games was raided by the police in 1958. In 1959, his mother escaped under the nose of the waiting press by being carried out in a laundry basket while one of England's greatest lords removed himself through a back window. By

1962, when the law had been changed, Aspinall decided to open a permanent place. His first club established a standard of decadence unequalled even by Monte Carlo during the Belle Epoque. At one of his parties, the staircase was festooned with dwarfs, while acrobats and wild animals roamed around the rooms. The guests were too drunk, or amazed, to be scared. All his parties were centred around a theme or around one of Aspers' heroes, people like Mithradates or the Diadochi or Cuauhtémoc, the last of the Aztecs. The expense and attention to detail at each feast were enormous. But so were the profits because Aspinall would take a percentage of every winning coup.

In 1970, the law changed once again. The new gaming act prohibited credit and forbade the owner to play in his own game. Nor could any drinks be served. Aspers decided to get out. He had already bought a famous house, a small but perfect Palladian structure called Howletts, near Canterbury. Since his first win, he had been stocking his house with wild animals. With his wife, Sally, born Curzon, he began breeding tigers, gorillas, rhinos, wolves, sable antelope, leopards, buffalo, and wild cattle. When his son Bassa was only six months old, Aspers put him in with his favourite gorillas. The baby was snatched up by a large female gorilla. Neither Aspers nor Sally minded.

Aspinall also began a wildlife preservation campaign. He hired the huge Albert Hall and gave speeches to rapt audiences. He wrote a book and became a very sought-after speaker. He spent $1 million a year for the upkeep of his animals. Naturally, he did not diminish his style of life, so he was soon in need of money. There was only one thing to do: go back to gambling.

He bought the lease of a smaller house on Sloane Street built in the nineteenth century. He decorated it in *fin-de-siècle* sumptuousness. The scene had, however, changed dramatically. Whereas in 1960, 90 per cent of the gamblers were English, in 1979, confiscatory taxes and the general decline of the English economy had made them as rare as dinosaurs. The Greeks were barely hanging on because a shipping slump was entering its fifth year. The only people who could afford to gamble big were the Arabs, the Persians, and the Nigerians.

Needless to say, the latter were interested only in women when not gambling. Almost every casino in London was running a call girl service in order to accommodate clients. Aspers, however, refused to do this. Not on moral grounds; he simply found it inelegant and plebian. But he captured many of the biggest punters anyway, simply by setting a very high maximum on a single blackjack box and by allowing up to $20,000 to surround a single number in roulette. The word got around. The place was soon full.

After an initial loss of about $3 million, Aspinall recovered and is at present operating in the black. His club once again has the best food in town and the best service. No gossip columnists are allowed to enter, so privacy and secrecy are ensured. There are private rooms where one can gamble with no one looking on. And there is an opportunity to make a fortune overnight. Or lose one. But as the famous zoologist Anthony Smith said: 'Never have gaming profits been put to better use.' Aspinall agrees. Sometimes when he sees one of his gambler friends complaining about a loss, he points to a picture of one of his tigers or gorillas and says, 'How would you like to see that beautiful beast go hungry? People with too much money can only relieve their boredom by risking it. Be happy. You are finally not bored.'

NAME DROPPING

My friend Rupert Pilkington-Boreham Wood is a very self-confident young man. He has never been known to touch his tie the way self-conscious people do when entering a room full of strangers. Nor does he ever cross his arms in front of his body in a defensive stance. Because of his aplomb Rupert is known among his friends as 'the chairman'. The chairman is in his early thirties, a man of medium height and fair complexion. The pinstripes he wears are as thick as the frame of his glasses.

The chairman is married to a pretty girl whom he treats with benign neglect at all times, like a gentleman should. I have known the chairman for about 12 years or more and I have always liked him. As of last year he has joined the pantheon of heroes I reserve for people like John Wayne, George Patton and Genghis Khan. All of them unfashionable in a world that falsely believes that fashion is the tide of history.

It was about a year ago that John Bowes-Lyon — Bosie to his friends as well as to Mark, Lola, Vitas, Bianca, and even Taki — was called upon by Halston, the transvestite-looking couturier who needs no introduction among gays and rich women, to organise and act as host to a public relations party at the Savoy.

Bosie, to his eternal credit, was not a smart organiser. Instead of inviting only people who read *Vogue* magazine, the kind who know the difference between Dru and Jack Heinz, he extended invitations to those Hooray Henrys that inevitably the chairman must uncharitably be considered to be part of. Rupert was rather surprised to receive an invitation. In fact he was so surprised he actually spoke to his wife. 'Nice of Bosie to invite us,' he said, grinning, 'the canapés are pretty good at the Savoy.'

The evening of the party it was raining as usual. Rupert, walking five feet ahead of his wife, advanced fearlessly into the grand ballroom and immediately headed for the buffet. That is when he ran across a tall, Dracula-like figure with a white pansy face and an imperious if rather effete manner. Bosie was standing next to him. The chairman greeted Bosie and then, remembering his wife's coat, he turned, took it from her, and thrust it in the imperious figure's outstretched hand. 'I am Halston,' said the elongated man, raising both eyebrows and turning whiter than usual. 'Thank you, Halston,' boomed the chairman, leaving the guest of honour holding the coat as he headed towards the caviar and canapés with the kind of relish exhibited by most people for anything free today.

Later on Rupert was seen flanked by his friends imbibing great quantities of champagne and protesting about the presence at the party of queers and foreigners. He was the last to leave after thanking Bosie for the food and drink. Although some might think that the chairman's behaviour was rude, I think the contrary. The chairman, you see, never knew what a

Halston was. Most of his friends have double-barrelled names, and the ones that don't have at least a Christian one to go with their surname. I realised how unfair all this was to the chairman only recently. I was having a drink with him last week at Annabel's, when two breathless groupies announced that they were about to have drinks at Mark and Lola's (the high priests of social mountaineering) in honour of Vitas. Rupert Pilkington-Boreham Wood got annoyed. 'In honour of Vitas?' he expostulated. 'How can anyone throw a party for a cereal?' he demanded.

The chairman was unaware that jet-set groupies only refer to their heroes by their first names in the time-honoured tradition of Hollywood name-dropping. He did not know that Vitas (Le Beau) Gerulaitis has become the latest catch name to be dropped, even though he didn't do too well at Wimbledon.

In a world full of groupies desperately trying to get a smile, a nod, a sign of recognition from a Warren, a Jack, a Liza or a Halston, it was reassuring as hell to know that there are still people around who last week thought that a Borg was a transmission. As Faulconbridge once said, 'This England never did, nor never shall, Lie at the proud foot of a conquering couturier.'

RICH GIRL

Gore Vidal, whose bitchiness makes Truman Capote resemble the saintly Hugh Fraser by comparison, once accused the Press of being involved in a conspiracy to protect the rich from extinction. The way he saw it was as follows: The Fourth Estate always depicts the rich as being unhappy, mixed-up and having a terrible old time. But, because of a Goebells-like brainwashing, the rich survive: i.e., if truth was really told — what a great time the rich in fact have always had — the poor would rise up and kill them all.

It is an interesting theory, probably the most compassionate thing Vidal has ever uttered, definitely the nicest. And, surprisingly, almost true. Although there is no conspiracy, it is a fact that the rich, like blondes, have more fun. That is because they have a choice. After all, as everyone knows, the difference between the unhappy rich and the unhappy poor is that the former can choose their kind of misery.

That was the case with the late Barbara Hutton. The oft-married Woolworth heiress reportedly spent much of her life searching for happiness, which eluded her. This was the stuff of which true Greek tragedy is born. Her attempt to bring meaning to her life, always according to the omnipotent Fourth Estate, involved a constant search for a perfect husband. I say rubbish. She found meaning in her life by indulging in every whim and being able to experience things far out of reach of the ordinary man or woman. This might sound corny or pedestrian to sophisticated Europeans, but Barbara Hutton was an American, naive, enthusiastic and dazzled by it all.

In the beginning she had the natural fascination many Americans have for nobility. She married into it five times. Her enchantment with Hollywood was satisfied by Cary Grant. Then she married probably the greatest sportsman, in the true sense of the word, Gottfried von Cramm. Finally, her curiosity about the jet-set (in those days the propeller set) was satisfied by her union with Porfirio Rubirosa, the archetypal macho-playboy. Yet her natural inclination was for the finer things in life. Her Chinese porcelain collection was one of the best, and her Japanese furniture the finest in quality outside Japan.

But all this was easy. It took taste and money. What required more than that was her ability to help people, artists mostly, and never ask for anything in return, and never get any recognition for it. How many so-called patrons of the arts can claim this? The only charitable work she was known for was her donation of the house in Regent's Park to the American government. Yet she paid for countless aspiring music students' education, contributed generously to the Free French during the war, and gave large gifts — like the great carpet of Marie Antoinette — to Versailles. None of the above was ever reported because she made sure it wasn't. She was secure enough not to need applause.

Where the Press in general and the gossip columnists in particular failed miserably was in their description of her person. Until 1960 she was an extraordinarily beautiful woman. She read all the time and wrote poetry. Unlike pseudo-intellectuals she never mentioned the fact. And the men in her life understood that here was a woman that could not be conquered with the standard good performance in bed. But she loved men, refined ones, and never was with one that would qualify for a full page spread of revelations in a Rupert Murdoch paper. Adventurers, yes; male Margaret Trudeaus, no.

Her only crime being that she was born rich, she will undoubtedly be remembered as something of a freak, a typical product of the capitalist system. No matter. She enjoyed her life more than most, and she had the best laugh. Living well is, after all, the best revenge.

TWO-TON TONY

In 1970, while solipsism reigned supreme among students of the Western world, and campuses burned down in protest against a war that could possibly curtail the drug and good times for an unfortunate few, a group calling itself Jocks Against The War In Vietnam came into being. The group was mostly made out of failed athletes, a large proportion of them 'gay', all of them taking overdoses of mind drugs and media exposure.

In view of the times the jock ploy for attention was not surprising. The fact, however, that athletes once expected to embody heroism and the finer things of life, had joined the great unwashed, Jane Fonda brigades, was. So, while Jane Fonda prepared to go to North Vietnam to give comfort to the people who were torturing American pilots, and get some pretty good publicity for herself, I went looking, like Diogenes, for an honest man. I found him in New Jersey, part of the silent majority but hardly silent. His name was Tony Galento; he died two weeks ago.

Galento was called 'The Grotesque Gladiator' but to the same newspapermen who labelled him that, Tony Galento was beautiful. He was a columnist's and cartoonist's dream, but not when the subject of war and war protesters came up. He was a poor boy who fought all his life to survive and had survived because of the classless American system, and hated the spoiled kids who thought America was the most fascist, oppressive country in the world. Galento hardly articulate, possessed the type of heroic virtue that today's modern psychologists and Marxist professors speak of as obsession or self-destructing. The last two years of life he suffered terribly. Both of his legs were amputated. Needless to say he never complained. He died without tears. Although I am a Christian there are times when I begin to doubt. Why should Galento have suffered?

The five foot nine inch roly-poly with the powerful left hook had a total of 114 fights taking on any and all comers from 1929 until 1944 when he called it a career with a three round KO win over Jack Suzek in Kansas City. Now, 40 years later, the image remains. Two-ton Tony Galento, a beer-bellied, beer-guzzling street fighter. It wasn't until 13 June 1935, when Galento was fighting in a prelim to the Jimmy Braddock -Max Baer title fight for the heavyweight championship of the world that he gained prominence. This was the night that Jimmy Braddock was to stun the world by taking the title away from the favourite. Galento fought a six foot six inch giant called Young Hippo. The bell sounded and the little round man came out swaggering. Wham. One left hook by two-ton Tony and Hippo was out cold. After that everyone kept away. Except for Louis.

The greatest ever gave Tony a title fight which no one took seriously. Except for Galento. Not that he trained for it. He kept up his drinking while announcing that he would 'moider da bum'. And he almost did. On 28 June 1939, the little round man, who, incidentally, was the first man to say 'I've brung the title back to Jersey', uncorked a beaut of a left hook which deposited the great Louis on the floor.

It proved to be his undoing, however, because Louis for the second time in his life got angry and hammered away like a man possessed. The referee had to stop it because Tony would not go down. He was bleeding from every part of his face. Afterwards in his dressing room, Galento said, 'I woulda licked him if I foughta de way I wanted but he wouldn't lemme.'

Two-ton Tony ran a bar until the end. He volunteered in the war, and became a wrestler afterwards. He once wrestled an octopus which died after a week. Tony felt embarrassed. He thought his manager had done the octopus wrong. He didn't keep much money, but enough to send his kids to a good school. When he became sick he refused welfare, or a testimonial charity affair. Two-ton Tony, who could have been champ if they had no Queensberry rules left a vivid impression on all men. He was beautiful.

14.   LABOUR PAINS: *Jeffrey Bernard*

JOB SATISFACTION

It occurrs to me that there is a sort of illness I don't have but
wish I did suffer from. I suppose it might be called acute
lexicographitis. It takes the form of a compulsion to cover
blank sheets of paper with words. Now, of course, it's a
wonderful thing to enjoy one's work, but lexicographitis in its
chronic form can lead to wealth, fame and success. Keith
Waterhouse is a typical sufferer. I can understand publicans
enjoying their work and yet they are sidetracked by trivialities
and spend far too much time discussing such subjects as
motorway systems and the weather and doctors adore just
everything about their work except for their patients. Then
there are those like George Best who love everything about
their work except the money and success which they just
can't take.

I remember two episodes which upset me some time ago
and they were two separate days on the booze, once with
Mick Jagger and on another occasion with Tony Hancock.
Jagger was alright to begin with — we spent all afternoon
after the pubs had closed in a grotty little club called the
Kismet — but he cracked at about 5 p.m. and he tearfully told
me that the money and fame was driving him mad. Yes, I
did suggest he unload some of it on to me but he didn't seem
attracted by the idea. You just can't help some people.

Then I met Hancock in the York Minster one morning at
opening time. We got talking, possibly because we were the
only two in the bar, and we spent the rest of the day together.

A lovely fellow but a casualty. (Pubs are casualty wards
aren't they?) By the early evening Hancock was legless. I
folded him into a taxi and he sat on the floor of it. From that
position he solemnly gave me his telephone number. Lying
down he said, 'Phone me sometime when you're in trouble.'
'I'm quite alright,' I said. 'No, I think you may have a drink
problem,' he said and then passed out.

Racehorse trainers are one bunch of people I know who love
their work and some of them get what almost seems like a kick
out of their disappointments. In that game too, bookmakers
like their work much as foxes must like eating someone's
chickens. But it's this writing nonsense that puzzles me.
What's more, there's a whole new breed of graduates coming
along into the Fleet Street arena who simply adore the idea of
assaulting blank sheets of paper. I seem to remember that *The
Sunday Times* or someone once did a survey asking under-
graduates what they most wanted to do when they left university and most of them said they wanted to be journalists
because it's terribly exciting and you get to *meet famous
people*. I ask you. What these people don't seem to realise is
that all work cuts into one's spare, idling, drinking and
kibbitzing time. One needs at least ten hours a day to look out
of the window. The idea that there's virtue in work for its
own sake needs knocking on the head once and for all.

Being a boss, pure and simple, is the guvnor job. Dele-
gation is something you can do standing on your head. Ideally
one should start at the top and the sort of man who tells you
that life is tough or lonely at the top needs shooting. The
alternatives are quite hideous. Keith's typewriter is probably
a water cooled contraption and his brain must be permanently
firing on all cylinders. Isn't it enough to sit about in pubs
conjecturing? I mean, there's no need to actually *write* about
all that stuff. All that really needs writing is cheques and
betting slips.

QUACKERY

In my desperation to get away from journalism I'm seriously
thinking of bluffing my way into entirely new fields of work.

My bad luck though stems from a very ordinary public school education which equipped me to do precisely nothing. Not one thing that held my interest in the classroom has been of any use to me since, and what I learned between lessons, manners and the foxtrot, is rusty and obsolete. So, I've been scanning the newspaper ads for vacancies and the only jobs I've come across that might possibly enable me to continue to live like an impoverished lord are those that I'll simply have to bluff my way into.

I'm tempted to apply for quite a few academic posts and they're crying out for lecturers in English Literature in the Middle East and darkest Africa. The way I see it, I'll set my students the task of reading something like *Middlemarch* and then ask them to write a 5,000-word essay on it, by which time I'll not only be tumbled and fired but will have been at it long enough to get a diamond handshake. Then, of course, everyone needs doctors in all those outbacks and I reckon, armed with a few text books and tools of the trade, I'd last a good three months — if not as a flying doctor then one with a taxi.

Ideally, I'd like someone to lend me a modest £10,000 so that I could open a bar restaurant by a West Indian beach; but as that's not to be — you fools — then it's got to be the gem of a job I saw advertised in *The Times* last week. It went like this. 'Postdoctoral Research Fellow. Applications are invited for a post of Postdoctoral Research Fellow to work on the computer-simulations of 10 — 10 eV cosmic-ray extensive air showers and to join an SRC-supported research group under the direction of Dr A.L. Hodson using a $42m^3$ array of current-limited spark chambers and a $3m^2$ cloud chamber to investigate sub-cores and high pt phenomena in air showers and to search for e/3 quarks near the shower axes.'

Well, that job just had to be a walkover — a complete doddle. I particularly like the idea of searching for the odd quark which is, as we all know, a cross between a duck and a dog and not to be confused with the Dog and Duck in Frith Street. I'm pretty sure that the crucial hours of this laboratory bluff would be those in the first day at work. There'd be

numerous introductions — lingering a little over those to my
female colleagues — and then I suppose Dr Hodson would let
me settle in to my bench or office before chatting me up over
the ubiquitous instant coffee. I can hear him now.

'Well. Doctor Bernard, tell me, why did you leave your
last post?' 'Funny you should ask that. Yes. Ha, ha. As a
matter of fact, and although I say it myself, it was due
entirely to professional jealousy.' 'Jealousy? How come?'
'Well, you see, I was finding so many quarks without even
going anywhere near the shower axes let alone using an almost
zero-rated, current-limited spark chamber that they simply
couldn't stand it. Mind you, I was glad to go and I'm glad to
be here where, I understand, I'll be able to work largely on
my own.' 'Quite.' 'Any more of that coffee before I roll my
sleeves up?' 'Yes, of course.' 'That reminds me. Is there
anywhere decent to eat lunch around here?' 'Well, we do have
a canteen which I'm sure you'll find amply . . .' 'Oh no. I like
to get away during the lunch hour. Never could stand shop
talk. Devoted as I am to research I wouldn't want to take a
quark with me to lunch. Ha, ha.' 'Quite.' 'Right, let's get at
those extensive air showers then. Hang on.' 'What is it
doctor?' 'I've just noticed the time. It's 12.30 already.'
'Indeed it is.' 'Well, we're in Cambridge aren't we. They open
at 10.30 here don't they?' 'They?' 'The pubs, old man. Come
on. You know what makes Doctor Jack a dull boy, don't you?'
'Well, er, yes. I suppose I could show you our immediate
environs if you wish it.' 'Come on then. Those sub-cores
wont't run away before closing time, will they?' 'No, I suppose
not, but I'm not sure we should be . . .'

For a few days I might just be considered a mad, eccentric
genius before the boot and a month's wages. But that would
just about tide me over until I started drilling for oil for BP
or lecturing in chemistry at Roedean.

CLOCKING ON

A heading in my local paper caught my eye last week, and that
takes some catching when it's the *Newbury Weekly News* in

pursuit. Usually, the headings concern gymkhanas, harvest festivals, Women's Institute happenings or spell-binding occurrences like a local council moving a bus stop fifty yards up the road. But this heading had me waxing more nostalgic than I felt since I last heard 'We'll Meet Again'. It said, 'Work-Shy Man Is Now A Reformed Character'. I liked it instantly and plunged on into the epic.

It seems that the character in question hit the headlines last year when he was taken to court for failing to maintain his wife and children. Apart from being work-shy, he couldn't hold down a job because he was so bad at time-keeping. The Department of Health and Social Security even offered to buy him an alarm clock to get him up in the mornings, which I thought was nice of them. Anyway, the second time he appeared in court he pleaded guilty to dishonestly using £3.92 worth of electricity. The Southern Electricity Board had previously cut off his supply when his arrears topped the £279 mark and he reconnected the stuff himself.

The defending counsel said that the defendant was now holding down a full-time job and that, 'he has undergone a complete transformation not only concerning large things like how to manage his finances but also little things like personal hygiene. The family's future looks better than it has done for some considerable time.' Finally, our character got two years' probation. Well, I ask you! It's a sad but piddling story and I am only sorry that I wasn't on or anywhere near the bench to offer my summing up.

First, I would like to take the phrase 'work-shy'. Now it may be because I have never been able to see the virtue of hard work *for its own sake* or it may be because I've very rarely had a job I've enjoyed, but at any rate I find it an extremely offensive phrase, used to label people who are either depressives, emotionally unstable in other ways or who have a simple objection to working at jobs like washer-upper, factory assembly line hand or shop assistant or any other bloody job that doesn't involve a three-hour lunch break that dissolves into an afternoon session in a club. If someone is just lazy then it's a pussy-footing phrase, like 'distressed gentlefolk' which simply means skint persons who talk proper.

The other thing that struck me about the case was that having used the phrase 'work-shy' defending counsel goes on to use the phrase 'holding down' a job. Now how can a man be shy of something he's holding down? For that matter why shouldn't a man be shy of something so horrendous that it has to be held down?

In any event I am glad I wasn't in court to sum up, for who on earth would want to be in a court where counsel and, presumably, bench and audience, hold personal hygiene to be such a little thing? Then, dismissing hygiene with a wave of an, I assume, incredibly grubby hand, counsel gave out the flannel about the family's fortune being better than it has been for some considerable time. Well, he's got to try and get his client off so we'll let him have his flannel, but will the future be so rosy? I doubt it.

LABOURING

There are times, and they're becoming more frequent, when being a hack gives me a pain in almost every part of my anatomy. For the past few weeks I've been struggling to think of alternative ways to make a living and I haven't been able to come up with a single idea. The only advantage I can see to this business is that it provides enough free time to pop out occasionally for 'just the one'; the only other job that does just that seems to be acting. It's a sad fact really that actors are dotted lines only joined up by the 3B pencil when they've working, otherwise they'd be able to enjoy the part of their lives that I so envy — resting. I can think of nothing nicer than being between engagements, assuming of course, the engagements themselves weren't too trivial. No, what I'd really like to be is a businessman. I don't mean the City variety, but something slightly more spivvy. Bloodstock agent appeals tremendously as does nightclub owner, restaurant owner — hours of delicious table-hopping driving the customers mad — or magazine editor of the glossy variety enabling me to delegate work to frightened people in pleasant surroundings.

I failed pretty miserably at my one and only business

venture and that was when I had a book barrow in Earlham
Street Market in the early Fifties. I managed to stock it in the
first place with unwanted books collected from various friends.
Bernard Kops had the barrow next to mine and Quentin Crisp,
I think I remember correctly, dabbled in antiques and jewellery
a few yards up the pavement. It was quite jolly. The trouble
was, my barrow — next to Tubby Isaacs's stall — was just
outside the pub by the corner of Cambridge Circus and when
I made a sale I'd pop in for a half of bitter. I sold a first edition
of a W.H. Auden once for the princely sum of ten shillings
and left the barrow unattended for three hours. You see, if
you're a businessman you really need to think beyond opening
time and concentrate on what women call 'the future'.

Perhaps the best thing for someone to do who's completely
untrained to do anything whatsoever is to tell other people
what to do or, at least, give them advice. Sidney Graham once
set up as an 'excuse-smith' selling ne'er-do-wells excuses for
ten shillings a time but the denizens of Soho became quite
good at it themselves and he had to revert to a different sort of
poetry. One thought that did strike me was to open a deli-
catessen in Lambourn, where there isn't a shop to speak of in
Fortnum's terms, and put a manager in it. Of course,
managers fiddle but 19-year-old female manageresses don't
and God knows why since most barmaids do. It would be
dreary I know but I quite like the idea of popping in once a
day to empty the till.

I suppose what I want is a job as brief as an assault on a
typewriter but one whose result is a little more secret. Professional punter I like the anxiety can last as little as 58
seconds at Epsom on a dry day, but we all know that luck goes
in cycles and I haven't got the stamina for cycling. The gigolo
is the one man I can think of who has to earn *every* penny of
his money and I'm too fond of clean sheets and baths etc to
ever be a layabout again. I've even thought of becoming a
complete drop-out but what park-bencher ever laid a woman?
('Would you like to come back to Hyde Park for a glass of
meths?') No, I suppose this will just have to go on. Sorry about
that.

AVERSION THERAPY

Last month I finished a six-week stint working as a barman in a club in Soho and the horror of the job worked wonders. Dispensing the stuff and listening to the dialogue that issued from the receptacles of it proved to be better therapy than anything I ever came across on a couch or at the point of a needle. Today makes it 24 weeks since I touched a drop and turned gamekeeper and the more I see of poachers the tighter I cling to my wagon.

Expert observers in the field of alcoholism might tell you that I'm going through the 'honeymoon period'. This is a phase of unduly over-optimistic thinking accompanied by the glow of having discovered a new world formerly hidden in the depths of a drunken haze. That's how my old doctor would describe it anyway and he'd have a good point but for the fact that he's never served drinks to actors and writers and TV producers and journalists and hustlers and lunatics from 5.30 p.m. until midnight and watched the wheels drop off them one by one on the way.

The evening always started off well enough. At opening time, glasses polished and lager at the cold and ready, I'd greet the first few customers and we'd talk in clichés for half an hour. 'Hard day at the office?' I'd ask and they would say something on the lines of 'Yes. Mustn't grumble. I see Boycott's got another century. What won the four o'clock? You must see *The Last Detail* if you haven't already.' Just like a pub in fact and that's the way it stayed for the first hour. At that point it was hard to believe that those same people would be talking gibberish and falling through their front doors before the night was out.

The first signs of aggravation would come at 8 o'clock when my best customer would have clocked up his sixth glass of wine. By best, of course, I mean worst. The man I'm talking about provides the voices for several TV commercials and half a lifetime spent in sound booths has given him the idea that what he says matters. He claims to be in constant touch with Albert Einstein but I think he's got his lines crossed and is in fact in touch with Pistol. He'd spend an hour needling me about my new-found sobriety and when he got tired of that it would be time for me to start conducting my own group therapy class.

My class consisted mainly of actors — a much maligned bunch of idiots — and like most drinkers they fell and fall into three main groups. There are 'Come outside and I'll smash your face in' ones, 'Nobody loves me' ones and a handful of manic 'Wouldn't it be fun to stand on our heads in Piccadilly Circus?' ones. Far the most common drunk is the 'Nobody loves me' one. Easy but tedious to listen to, an hour of him makes you long for a nice, quiet, introverted drug addict. 'Nobody loves me' plays with his self-pity like a dog with a bone. He goes on very much like the mother who's forever telling her children what she sacrificed to get them where they are and who then adds not to worry about silly old her, she'll be all right.

'You don't know what it's like,' he tells you staring at a wet patch on the counter and you don't bother to contradict him.

'You don't know what true despair's all about. Jesus, I could tell you. Ever woken up skint and alone and known that that night you'll still be alone?'

You don't answer. You just look interested and continue dusting a bottle of Chateau Filth.

'I may not be Leonardo da Vinci and perhaps I don't look much like Paul Newman but when I think of some people and what they're doing . . .'

'Yes, I know.

'I mean, is there something wrong with me?'

'Of course not.'

'Well, you tell me. I dunno. Christ, how girls can actually fancy that bloody Jim. He must have money. I'll have another scotch in there. Yes, it all comes down to loot in the end. You know what my wife said to me?'

'What?'

'My bloody wife. She said your trouble — my trouble, my bloody trouble was her — she said your trouble is that you're living in a dream world. Marvellous isn't it?'

'Yes.' (You can't call anyone 'sir' after that lot.)

'Oh well. To hell with them. At least I haven't sold out,'

he says defiantly and you resist the temptation to tell him that's because he hasn't had any offers. 'I'll meet the lot of them on the way down. Actually, I've never said this before but you're a bit like me.' That's a cheek but you just say, 'Oh?'

'Yes. You don't give a damn, that's why you're a barman. I worked behind a bar once. Never again. The crap that drunks come out with. Christ. I expect you've noticed it?'

'A bit.'

'Some people think the world owes them a living. I'm not drunk by the way, but I'll tell you one thing mate. When they're down, kick 'em. It's the only way. You take my wife. You know her, don't you?' (You have, you do and you've discussed him with her so you go on dusting the bottle.) 'She only likes winners. Can't stand a loser. I know she's put up with a lot — even talked about leaving me once. Ha.' He pauses to smile indulgently at the folly of it and the very idea of anyone actually leaving good old him. 'Mind you, I've had my fair share of crumpet. Who hasn't?'

Me, you think reaching for the Perrier water.

'I can't put it down on paper but *I* could tell you a story. Listen, I've had a fantastic life. D'you know, my family . . . the misery. No, listen. Have I ever told you about my mother?'

'Yes.'

'My mother, a remarkable woman in many ways, my mother was potty. Stark raving mad. When I was six. No, seven. Wait a minute, six. Yes, I would have been six. Do you know what she did? She . . .'

He bears a cross and loves the tragedy of it all.

The truth is that what he and the wife of another boozer can't bear is my making any remark about the business of drink that's slightly ribald. It's in bad taste they say, and start looking hurt.

Well if I can't laugh at it who can? Of course it's tragic and don't I know. Don't talk to me about tragedy, I could tell you a thing or two. If only I could put it down. Did I tell you about . . .

15. THE PALACES AND PLAYPENS OF THE RICH: *Taki*

FRENZIED

New York

Imagine an airline hangar decorated by Salvador Dali, all nightmarish mauve, blue strobe lights flashing, crimson neon tubes blinking, punk-chic disco music blasting. Add people writhing in smart tuxes, Sassoon trims and Yves St Laurent evening dresses. This is Studio 54, the most fashionable discotheque in New York. Just off 8th Avenue on 54th street, it is located only four blocks off the DMZ — where teenage hookers and their pimps ply their trade.

The place began as a cinema and later served as a television studio. Today its structure remains unchanged. A large foyer, a great central room and a lofty amphitheatre. Muscular, half-naked bartenders rock to the music while serving drinks in the circular bar. Up above couples watch the dancing, sway to the music or make love in the aisles. A mix of raw sensuality and of intensity pervades. Walking around the place is like reading a gossip column when stoned.

There is Andy Warhol, a picture of contrived dishevelment, surrounded by Scott and Zelda Fitzgerald types. Warhol never speaks, never drinks, just keeps watching. Bianca Jagger pops some pills and goes into a frenzied dance with Halston, the designer. Halston is a Dracula-like figure, elongated, mysterious and aloof. Unlike Dracula, however, he prefers to sniff white things than suck the traditional red stuff from the necks of maidens. Over in the bar Walter Cronkite sips Diet-Rite Cola.

Given the fact that New Yorkers are the greatest snobs

and social climbers in the world, Studio 54 and the attitude that goes with it is more than just a social fly-by-night phenomenon. It has been described as a revolutionary gesture by the rich and the haves who have been pushed around by hip minorities for too long. No more slumming in Harlem, tea-dances for the black panthers or mixing with the freaks. Wall Street, Park Avenue and the top echelons of the media have turned punk-chic and the blacks, the freaks and the crazies are outside looking in.

This is Studio 54's contribution to contemporary history. It has accomplished more in a year than thousands of shrinks at 200 dollars per hour have in a generation. The man who liberated New York society from its anxieties and constant social climbing is a twenty-eight-year-old Jewish boy from the Bronx, a Yale graduate called Steve Rubell. He began with hamburger stands, graduated to hamburger restaurants and then hit upon the idea of Studio 54. His thinking was simple. Instead of down-marketing for the rich, or up-marketing for the middle, why not down-market the product but up-market the people. In other words separate the ritzy from the rich and the trendy from the trendies.

The result was that he is now considered to be in New York what Mrs Vanderbilt was a generation ago. A social arbiter. A creator of society. But instead of having only 400 (that's all she could squeeze in for dinner) Rubell has one thousand. How does one make it inside? How does one qualify? There are no set rules for acceptance but a plethora of them for rejection. For example: two gold chains around one's neck, three-inch heels for men, platform shoes for women will make one as welcome as a pork chop at a kosher dinner. Double knits ditto. Out are fat executive types, no matter how rich and that includes all Arabs.

Social observers admit that it was about time. What was perversely cast as society until today in New York was a bunch of demented Protestants known as Wasps who posed as Englishmen by wiring their jaws together and trying to speak in what became known as Park Avenue lock-jaw. On which subject, Jackie Onassis, the undisputed queen of New York café society, tried at first to resist Steve Rubell. When she saw that he was too strong she attempted to bowl him over. She failed on both counts. She now pays homage to him by attending regularly and never asking for special privileges.

It is not difficult to understand the Studio 54 philosophy and why it has caught on. Lacking a language whose inflections can suggest precise points on the social spectrum and their attendant values, New Yorkers have always relied on nightclubs for identity. But nightclub owners have throughout the ages let them down by preferring South American and Italian gigolos (as during the 'Forties and 'Fifties), blacks and hippies (as in the 'Sixties), Greeks and Arabs in the early 'Seventies. Now all this has changed. And you don't even have to drink a lot to belong. Steve passes out Quaaludes like Kleenex in a 'flu epidemic and there is no charge.

EAGLE EYED

Gstaad

The *sine qua non* of survival among snobs is — naturally — exclusivity. In the rarefied atmosphere of the Alps this clannishness takes the form of the private lunch club. It was created for the express purpose of protecting members from rubbing elbows with fellow skiers during lunch-time ingestion. There are only two such clubs in Europe, or in the European Alps rather: the Corviglia in St Moritz, and the Eagle Club in Gstaad.

As both St Moritz and Gstaad began crawling with people rich and poor on ancestry, a semblance of respectability was needed to bolster their unique creations. A search for snobs was initiated. The younger Eagle Club was lucky. It found a stray English lord and made him its first president. The much older Corviglia had to content itself with Italian titled folk, or worse, Greeks on its committee, and as both are a dime-a-dozen, the club — understandably — assumed a much snobbier pose.

The Earl of Warwick, Fulke to his friends, was the Eagle's lucky catch in 1957. Warwick used to be a St Moritz habitué until he clashed with some very rich but horribly vulgar late arrivals in the Grisons. Moving to Gstaad, he built a chalet and accepted the presidency. With him came Le Vicomte Benoist d'Azy, a French nobleman who used to run the Corviglia Club.

Being less of a climber than most Greeks, I chose Gstaad as my winter base of operations after graduating from school twenty-two years ago. I was invited to join the Eagle Club the year it opened by the Earl of Warwick himself. It was a riotous all-night party which probably had something to do with his decision. After thirty-three whisky sours he was convinced I was English and had been to Eton with him. The Vicomte was also in favour of my election. I was the first Greek he had ever met who spoke foreign languages. Soon after I joined the Eagle Club someone had the bright idea of holding a moonlight party. This consists of revellers taking a chairlift up the mountain around eight in the evening, imbibing, or rather decimating the Eagle's wine cellar, and finally skiing down by torchlight.

On my first moonlight party my friend Yanni Zographos, the nephew of the man who broke the bank at Monte Carlo, had one of his usual bright ideas. He ordered a Palace Hotel chef to make three enormous cakes consisting only of cream. The plan was to use the chef's creations as projectiles. Our target was Karim Aga Khan, recently enthroned as Aga and taking himself extremely seriously. Unknown to us, the Aga was accompanied at the party by a British diplomat attached to the United Nations in Geneva; he was a rather common-looking chap and we mistook him for one of the Aga's relatives. After a few drinks we attacked: in a matter of seconds both august gentlemen were covered in cream.

The Aga, a prudent man, said nothing. The diplomat took umbrage, came over to our table and yelled for us to stop. I threw another cake at him point blank, but he grabbed my arm and flipped me over the table in a classically executed judo throw. As I was going down, however, and despite my surprise at his very undiplomatic knowledge of that particular sport, I hooked his leg and brought him down with me. That is when the trouble started. Zographos, running over to separate us, struck the Englishman's eye with his ski boot.

It looked simply awful. Two foreign bullies against a poor diplomat. His eye looked even worse. Warwick and the Vicomte were crestfallen.

After a lot of shouting and long hours of committee meetings, the president and the Vicomte took pity on us and suspended us for one season. Fulke Warwick retired soon after that. The Vicomte became president but he is retiring next month and there are elections. I am a candidate against a French duke and a Swiss banker. I am sure to get two votes, the other one from Zographos.

TABLE MANNERS

Gstaad

The international set's ruling committee recently met here in emergency session and after a two-hour deliberation made it official: a whiff of intellectuality at the dinner table is worth at least two ex-monarchs, four members of Parliament or eight ambassadors. The committee's decision was not surprising in view of the fact that oil-rich invaders had cornered the market and that most gems, yachts, chalets, private jets, Hollywood actresses and private islands have ended up, like the Dorchester Hotel, in Arab hands. The emergency session was called when the social-climbing Dutch wife of a Belgian baron-banker gave a dinner in this beautiful Alpine village and managed to land only two Englishmen. Everyone else it seems refused to attend because of an Arab holiday.

By upgrading intellectuality into the most coveted status symbol, the leaders of the Beautiful People have shown a perspicacity rarely suspected of them. They have curtailed the suicidal status race which was draining everyone's resources, and deftly swept aside the Arabs who had unfairly ruined the market by overpaying everything from chalets to ex-monarchs to Hollywood starlets in that order. (The oil-rich invaders have refused to join the intellectual-for-dinner race as they deem the eggheads to be a unique Western perversion.)

One resort that has cried foul over the decision, however, is St Moritz. Chalet-dwellers there claim to have been dis-

criminated against. They point out that their town — also full
of overpriced hotels and very old people with new money —
had no room left for intellectuality. Ira von Furstenberg was
one indignant hostess who allowed her opinions to be known.
'We are not prepared for it. We have never seen an intellectual. How on earth can we compete with Gstaad under such
conditions? The only man we have here who could possibly
qualify is Stavros Niarchos. He does not know how to read but
can count up to one thousand million.'

This is not the case with Gstaad. Because of strict zoning
and building laws the place has retained the unspoiled quality
of a small Swiss village. And due to such qualities intellectuals
came here in droves. In fact, they managed to pass relatively
unnoticed for the better part of thirty years. But as soon as
the committee pronounced them desirable, about ten savants
were fought over by one hundred of Gstaad's social-climbing
hostesses. There was not enough intellectuality to go around.
Things became desperate. Wild-eyed German industrialists'
wives actually began grabbing unsuspecting skiers by the
collar. After a few unpleasant incidents the mayor of Gstaad
saw it as his duty to inform certain ladies that the dialect
spoken here among the farmers was not Latin, and that the
smell of cowdung does not necessarily mean art. (Jet-setters,
unfortunately, still think of intellectuals as poor, bearded
figures always scratching and throwing bombs.)

Nevertheless, the first victory went to a German. The lucky
lady bagged the hottest celebrity among the thinking set,
William F. Buckley, Jr. He is one of the most polite people on
earth but having him to dinner always presents certain
problems. He does not charge a fee for attending (unlike
Kenneth Galbraith) but insists on a piano, a harpsichord,
book-lined walls and an easel. The hostess provided all that
and bragged about it afterwards. The result was catastrophic.
Lorries were hired to bring grand pianos and portable libraries
to the village and traffic to a standstill. Buckley retired to the
Rougemont cemetery where he lives and refused any more
dinners. J.K. Galbraith seized the opportunity and has become
almost as good a dinner catch because of his availability and
easy credit terms.

As the word spread other intellectuals started to come out of the woodwork. They were not in the Buckley-Galbraith class but neither were they as demanding. Yehudi Menuhin's only requirement was for home-grown, macrobiotic food and an Indian yoga master to cleanse him after dinner. David the easiest catch in town and charming as usual, only asked for Prince Rainier and Princess Grace to be included as he has not left their side since their marriage.

Painters, sculptors, writers and even journalists showed up. If Buckley got a hostess ten points, *Newsweek*'s chief foreign correspondent, Arnaud de Borchgrave, got her one. Borchgrave would have fetched more (he is a count to boot) except for his annoying habit of first-name dropping. ('Anwar told me in Aswan last week, Zbig was saying in Washington yesterday, Henry called this morning, Jimmy advised me to go . . .')

As the height of the winter season approaches Cadonau's, the leading bookstore is doing overflow business. Every book by Buckley, Galbraith, Niven and Menuhin has sold out long ago. (Jet-setters do not actually read them but walk around with them, ski with them, go to parties with them.)

Things are so desperate that even Julie Andrews's book on things metaphysical is selling. In fact it is even worse. An unreadable book, *The Greek Upheaval*, was sold to Roman Polanski who sent for it from California, as his other commitments prevent him making his usual trip to Gstaad this year.

REGINE'S WAY

High lifers have been in an uproar since last week. Not unlike their counterparts on the other side of the Atlantic, at the United Nations, jet-set play-persons and other fashionable creatures of the night have been speculating and arguing over last week's exceptional events.

Briefly, the dispute among the Beautiful People is whether Regine's latest venture on the top of the old Derry and Tom's store in Kensington High Street will be a success or not. Will Regine take over London as queen of the night? Or will she go

the way of Bennett's, Dial 9, Le Privé and Wedgies: alive but
moribund.

To judge by the opening night confusion would be unfair.
There were flamingos roaming in the vast hanging gardens
and Shetland ponies trying to be squeezed into the lifts along
with Caroline Grimaldi and Philippe Junot. There were
heavies beating up ambassadors and waiters trying to kiss
Sylvester Stallone. There was Bernard Lanvin, a French
perfume-maker and terrible snob (he hates the idea that his
parents went into trade rather than something more acceptable
to the nobs), walking around with raised eyebrows and a
Gallic scowl only to be mistaken for a gay giving a come-on
and shoved into the lavatory by an aggressive queen. The
rest of the celebrity-props who are *de rigueur* for an opening
were also there: Jack Nicholson, Joan Collins, the obligatory
newscaster from the BBC, and, of course, Mark and Lola. (The
former being nice to an acid-pen gossip writer and then
spoiling it all by comparing him to an investment.)

In the middle of it all, a flame-haired Regine was as cool and
imperturbable as a German Panzer commander fighting the
French. She saw that everyone got a hello, that old clients
got a kiss and that the press was given what it was there to get,
free booze and very little information. Gossip columnists
were fawned upon more than the couple from Monaco, who
were busy denying rumours that they accept payments for
attending shindigs.

Helping Regine to draw the Beautiful People was Dido
Goldsmith, a girl who is about to displace Florence Grinda as
high priestess of the jet-set. Dido, amazingly even got John
Aspinall to attend the opening, a feat unheard of in the annals
of seduction. Aspinall simply hates nightclubs and people who
throw away their money on booze when they could either
gamble it or feed it to wild animals.

Twenty years ago, starting with almost nothing, Regine was
given a small piece of the action in an obscure nightclub in the
south of France after dancing the 'twist' there non-stop. She
has never looked back since. She has, however, always remembered her first benefactors and clients. One can go away for
years, come back to a new club with an impressive façade,

but always find the same waiters and the same Regine greeting you as if you were her most important customer. Despite the Arab onslaught and the money they throw around, Regine still tries to keep a few Europeans in her clubs for show.

The last thing that will probably make Regine's a success, but somehow the most important, is that London is a major tourist centre without a nightclub for the tourist. Annabel's will turn them away, so will Tramp's. Anything else is not worth going to. Regine's will fill the need. Universally known, she will probably be decorated one day for helping the balance of payments. She could even become a Dame.

ROSEY FUTURES

What do the King of Belgium and Rainier of Monaco have in common except claims to royalty? And what is the common denominator between the Duke of Kent, Alexander of Yugoslavia, Vittorio Emmanuele of Italy, Fouad Farouk of Egypt and Winston Churchill (grandson), except for titles? Finally, with the exception of money, what links a Rockefeller with a Rothschild, two Niarchoses with five Khashoggis, a Yamani with a Radziwill, and a Metternich with the ex-head of the CIA, Richard Helms?

The answer should be very easy, especially for snobs who make it a point to know where their favourite name-drop went to school. Because all the names represent alumni of Le Rosey school of Rolle and Gstaad, Switzerland. Unlike plebian places of learning like Eton, stuck for ever next to Windsor Castle, Le Rosey has two campuses: one for spring and autumn, the other for winter.

The school takes its name from the Chateau de Rosey, built in the fifteenth century and rebuilt in the eighteenth. Ninety-eight years ago a Swiss educator came upon the brilliant idea of creating a school for the foreigners who seemed about to overrun Switzerland. Monsieur Paul Carnal (no pun intended) bought the old chateau and on its fine park built new buildings modelled on the old. Le Rosey was half-way between Geneva and Lausanne, close to Lake Léman and even closer to the gnomes of Zurich. The original curriculum was a commercial type of course that prepared the future rich to learn to read a balance sheet. After Monsieur Paul's son, Henri, took over, the school became stiffer academically, but was still a 'country club' by comparison to others.

Taking a gamble Monsieur Henri bought a chalet in Gstaad during the first world war, and for a lark took the boys up for a season's skiing. They have been there every winter since. And now there are five chalets, seven mountains and twenty ski-lifts to keep the winter doldrums away. In 1932 the then Shah of Iran sent his son and heir to Le Rosey. He hoped some of the lustre would rub off on him as he (the father) had only recently become emperor. (He was, I believe, a sergeant before that.) The old Shah was right. The young Pahlavi, as he was called by everyone, not only became the top athlete of Le Rosey, he was also elected captain of the football team and head of the student council. A contemporary, Alexi de Rede, recalls that his rank had nothing to do with his election. 'Everyone thought he was a *parvenu*. And he was. But he earned all the honours he received.'

Rainier of Monaco was remembered as a shy young man who liked singing. Alistair Horne, the noted historian, does not agree. 'He looked frightfully *avant garde* wearing a bow tie in 1938,' says Horne. 'And always seemed even then about to say *rien ne va plus*.' Horne describes his four years at Le Rosey as traumatic. 'I picked up all my prejudices there. My American room-mate was the first man I heard say something nasty about Jews. I never knew one existed till then. I also learned to eat an eclair with one hand and, worst of all, picked up the habit of living above my capabilities.'

Alistair Horne was not the only one to be traumatised. Lord Brabourne left Eton because he had trouble breathing through his nose from a rugger injury. His first day at Rosey he was punched on the nose by Horne and his proboscis has never been the same since.

Most Englishmen who attended Le Rosey used the excuse of asthma. The Duke of Kent was one, the Earl of Suffolk and Berkshire another. The real reason was something else, but both have recovered since being exposed to Le Rosey's neighbourhood schools. At one time there were seventeen girls' colleges in a radius of fifty kilometres.

The training one got at Le Rosey was, needless to say, immeasurable. One learned to live with royals, the rich, and the whims of both. Peter Zervudachi, a Cairo-born Greek, is a perfect example. He tells his story with the kind of insouciance affected by people F. Scott Fitzgerald once described as 'different from you and me'. 'It was in Cannes around 1948. The game was poker, five-card draw. I had three aces, later drew the fourth. I bet the limit. Roughly £10,000. Farouk saw my bet. He had four kings. Counting himself it made five. He took the pot.'

CLUBLAND

New York

The disco war of New York heated up and exploded this week. The three major powers of disco — Studio 54, Xenon and Regine's, each using the same battle plan — tried for outright victory in a Dionysian orgy of free drinks, drugs and sex. The war of the discos is over the Core, the roughly 1,000 strong, mostly bisexual Quaalude and coke brigade that makes or breaks a place. The disco that attracts the Core is the undisputed numero uno. For the last year Studio 54 was king. And its diminutive, self-admitted homosexual owner, Steve Rubell, the most powerful man since Frank Costello. But his three-million-dollar profit of last year inspired Xenon.

Xenon means strange or stranger, or mysterious, in Greek. The game plan was to create a place with the craziness of Studio 54 and the comfort of Regine's. The co-owner is Peppo Vanini, a Swiss-Italian who has been successful in running nightclubs in Europe, mainly the Kings Club in St Moritz. Vanini decided to sink Rubell by taking over the old Henry Miller Theater on West 43rd Street and installing more gimmicks than *Star Wars* and *Close Encounters* combined, like a shooting gallery, three dimensions of neon, activated by laser beams, shot from the balcony.

But there is more than just gimmicks needed to capture the

Core. This is done by special parties thrown by the discos for the Core. Xenon fired the first shot this week — recognised even by old-time social observers as the frenziest ever — by inviting 750 beautiful people to honour Marisa Berenson's return from an unsuccessful marriage to a Los Angeles gangster but a successful plastic surgery on her face following a car accident. As Marisa entered a giant screen flashed a picture of her cuddling her baby, who already looks like George Raft. Marisa swooned with delight, the crowds outside threw plastic bags of excrement in fury at being outside. Truman Capote kissed the guest of honour and declared her 'The worst actress but best kept middle-age girl of the year.' The paparazzi had a field day.

Rubell counter-attacked by giving a birthday party. The Press, the Arts, the jet-set, café society and every rich queen in New York was invited. After caviar and champagne the BPs were taken by bus to the Studio. A seven-foot cake in the shape of a Quaalude was wheeled in while thousands of streamers and confetti rained down. Fifteen hundred gay voices sang 'Happy birthday to Steve' and then . . . pop went the giant cake-pill and out popped a half-naked Negro woman who, at closer inspection, turned out to be Bianca Jagger. She threw her arms up in the air like a triumphant boxer while five gee-stringed waiters climbed on top and carried her down. Rubell was visibly touched. He took the microphone and offered everyone Quaaludes. There was a riot and the goons were called in.

Last but not least came Regine. 'I do not compete with those clowns,' she told me. 'I run a reputable house. I will not allow drugs and rampant homosexuality in my place. If a couple want to make love, they can always go up to my apartment.' Regine gave a charity ball for Vitas Gerulaitis's favourite charity. At 500 dollars a ticket, she collected 100,000 dollars to teach under-privileged children tennis. Regine was ecstatic. 'Not only we got good publicity but helped all those people in Harlem to learn to play tennis,' she said. But a friend of mine expressed doubt: 'The way this city is going the money could wind up buying the purest Peruvian instead of tennis lessons.'

Still, it was a good week.

STUDIOUS

New York

Two years after taking New York by storm, the most successful nightclub in recent history has gone the way of the Labour government. In New York, where people take these things extremely seriously, the demise of Studio 54 has everyone talking. 'It's worse than Watergate,' was the way one Australian journalist working for *Time* magazine put it.

Studio 54, the club everyone aspired to be part of for so long, has been taken over by the bisexuals from the Bronx, the would-be beautiful people, the Biancas from the suburbs, and all the other twitchy-nosed nocturnal low-lifers who used to lay fruitless siege to its doors. To say nothing of the occasional full-fledged polyester duo from Cleveland or Atlanta.

Their vigil is now over. Soon they will be able to join the freaks, transvestites, groupies and professional gays who at present are masquerading as the in-crowd at Steve Rubell's version of capitalist decadence. Because the in-people, the crowd that does not rely on PR men to place their names in tomorrow's gossip columns, has been staying away from the place as if it were Cambodia. In the world of disco, however, which vibrates to the sound of an eternal Saturday Night Fever and where an ingenious hype machine has lobotomized all but the most discerning, the news that a place is no longer 'in' travels slowly. The change comes as subtly as the ageing process: by the time the not-so-beautiful ones find out, the glitterati are long gone. Then the game begins all over again elsewhere. Carrot, stick, hope, humiliation, and finally disappointment. Ironically, a disco makes its greatest profits when the slobs are allowed in at last. This is the case with Studio 54 today.

In a town where celebrity-watching takes precedence over sex, the demise of Studio 54 is quite an accomplishment. And it has to do with its Führer, the diminutive kid from Brooklyn who looks like Peter Lorre but once he was successful began acting like Humphrey Bogart: Steve Rubell. It also has to do with the fact that New Yorkers, who are known as the most masochistic people on earth after the British, suddenly would not take it any longer. They were insulted, pushed and beaten up too often. One man lost a testicle while being thrown out. He is a man of sixty and was caught in the middle of a fracas. A well-known physician, Dr Louis Rogow is suing the club after having his jaw broken by a bouncer and a well-known actress received multiple bruises but filed no charges.

None of these problems, however, was the catalyst that forced the people who count to move. All nightclubs are steeped in louche glamour, and the Studio's excesses only helped its image. Rubell's high-handed ways are a different matter. His bare-chested, athletic barmen wear satin shorts and are personally hired by him after a close examination. Needless to say they are rude to customers.

Rubell's Quaalude intake is legendary, but doesn't help when it comes to making friends. One mini-celebrity who continues to attend Studio 54 is the designer Halston. The elongated, Dracula-like figure has a propensity for the young and is rewarded with introductions. In turn he brings in Bianca and her crowd. But the European contingent, probably as instrumental as anyone in making a nightclub the place to be, have all for the last month been going nightly to Xenon. Xenon combines the craziness of Studio 54 with the luxury of Regine's. No-one has as yet lost a testicle at Xenon. And no-one should be surprised at the demise of 54. It was a microcosm of New York and the jet-set. Here today, gone tomorrow.

16. KNICKERS ON THE CEILING AND OTHER ROMANTIC TALES: *Jeffrey Bernard*

OVER AND OUT

'It's over,' she said. 'You've snapped at me for the last time. As far as I'm concerned, anything there was is finished.' I didn't say a word. For one thing I'd seen it coming and for another I was too tired to protest. I'd already thrown in the towel. I just stood there in the doorway and let her get on with it. 'We can go to the cinema if you like — we can go dutch — but as far as anything else is concerned, it's over.'

She waited for me to say something, but I didn't. I stood there thinking of about six different things at once. The end of the affair concentrates the mind wonderfully. The lurch in my stomach was already dying and like a man watching a pile of crockery falling in slow motion, I'd come to accept the crash even before she turned the door handle. Then she said: 'Aren't you going to say anything?'

I couldn't. I was miles away. The business about going dutch had really got me. I had a vision of us drifting around London going in and out of cinemas and restaurants, and me always saying to the management: 'Look, do you mind if we have separate bills? You see, we don't sleep with each other any more.' As well as that, I was thinking how very hard she was going to be to replace. She still stood staring at me, and her brown eyes were flecked with malice and realistic thinking.

I could have hugged her. I was like the dog that you kick that still gives a few involuntary wags of its tail as it creeps off into a corner. You might know that strange thought process. It's got nothing to do with arrogance or conceit, it's simply a dull amazement at the fact that someone can't see how truly wonderful you are. There you are, standing right in front of them like the never-to-be-repeated offer of a lifetime, in your prime and only a short climb away from your peak, and the fools can't see it. For a split second I regarded her with the pity I might extend a man who's forgotten to post a winning pools coupon and then she said: 'Well?'

I still couldn't think of anything to say that was going to be memorable enough to haunt her for the rest of her days so I put on my mask of tragedy and went through the usual motions of offering up the late, late prayer. It's one I mutter to myself constantly in betting shops and it goes 'Let's start again. I know I've been a fool, but if this horse wins the last race I promise I'll never have another bet again. Ever. Anyway, not until Saturday.'

So I stood there hoping I looked like something on the lines of the stag at bay, but fearing I was more like a poodle at bay and all the time she was seeping out of the room. By the time she got to be standing on the landing she was probably thinking about whether she'd picked up a parking ticket, and there I was trying to come up with something to keep my options open.

Then she spoke for the last time. 'So, it's goodbye then.' I couldn't even return her goodbye. I stood there and suddenly I saw that picture that I hadn't seen since my schooldays of Napoleon on the deck of the *Bellerophon* saying farewell to Europe, only it was me. Actually, it was more of a post-Charing Cross for me than a post-Waterloo. I was upset — no one likes their sweets to be taken away — but I wasn't heartbroken. There was a pain in my chest that was simply remorse but I wasn't able to summon a tear that would have reflected very well by the light on the landing.

Then she shrugged her mouth and left. As she did so I found myself thinking that it's just like it is in novels. People really do 'turn on their heels' when they go. I watched her go down the stairs and out of sight and then I heard the front door close. I went into the kitchen and put the kettle on, and as I stood there watching it I heard her nasty, tinny little Renault starting up. I waited for her to crash the gears. She didn't.

It's bloody fantastic, I thought, while I made some tea.
After a scene like that she remains so ice cold that for once
she doesn't make a mess of the gears. I mean, I ask you,
would a man remain so utterly cool after closing such a rhap-
sodical chapter in his life? Lordy, lord no. He'd drive straight
into a wall blinded by tears at a moderately safe 15 miles an
hour and she, if she had any heart at all, hearing the crash
of a smashed windscreen, would run down the stairs and out
into the street deliciously blaming herself.

I took my cup of tea into the sitting room and sat there
wondering at my own coolness. I felt strangely ashamed at
not being more upset so I put some Mahler on the record
player to see if that would provoke the appropriate misery.
Nothing. In fact, I sat there listening to the syrup feeling
distinctly irritated. She'd be on the phone now, I thought,
to an old friend. There's always an old friend lurking in the
background, you know. God, how I hate those old friends.
Usually it's a terribly reliable, pipe-smoking old friend —
who's never laid a finger on the lady in question, of course
— and who lectures at some obscure university on Anglo-
Saxon pottery, and you can't get much more decent than that,
and he's just waiting for your affair to go on the rocks. Up till
then he's been hanging around like a non-functioning lighthouse, but as soon as you do go on the rocks he suddenly
lights up. Nearly all women have gone one of these men they
keep for rainy days and these men, damn them, have *always*
got enough money to take the ladies out and cheer them up
over a very expensive dinner.

They'll be half way through the artichokes at this very
minute I thought as Mahler moaned in every corner of the
room. I could just hear them, never mind see them. 'No,
actually, I was very fond of him, Bob,' she'd be saying.
They've all got reliable names like Bob. 'But it's just that he
needs more love than I can possibly give him.' 'I know,
darling,' Bob would be saying while at the same time catching
the wine waiter's eye, filling a pipe with St Bruno, grinding the
pepper mill over madam's artichoke and scribbling a note
about a new find of 6th-century cocoa mugs near Winchester.

'Yes, I really was very attached to him,' she'd go on while

wiping that delicious mouth of hers with a napkin. 'It's just that I couldn't take any more of his snapping.' 'I know, I know,' Bob would say. 'But you must have known it couldn't last.' They always say that, as though they're bloody fortune tellers. 'I could tell he was trouble from the moment I met him,' Bob would say cleaning the blackboard chalk from under his nails with a toothpick. 'Come on. Have some more wine, old girl,' he concluded, putting a horrible, strong, dry, reassuring hand over hers.

The Mahler came to an end and by this time the waiter would have brought Bob the bill and he'd pay for it in new notes plucked from a crocodile-skin wallet. 'What you need, my dear, is a good night's sleep,' he'd be saying while pulling her chair away, helping her on with her coat and brushing breadcrumbs off his lousy, reliable Harris tweed sports jacket. 'I don't know what I'd do without you,' she'd say, being shepherded into a taxi. 'Just try to forget all about him,' Bob would be saying, pressing a crisp pound note into the lovable, cockney taxi driver's hand, and off she'd go valiantly, wiser and happier into the future.

All that happened exactly one year ago. I haven't seen her since, the Mahler's well scratched now and I've licked my wounds clean. Then yesterday she had the cheek to phone me up and ask me did I know of a good plumber? Some people have got not sensitivity whatsoever.

GOOD GIRLS

I was quite fascinated to read about the man who got a divorce because his wife wouldn't make love to him more than twice a week mainly because the court put so much emphasis on the fact that she'd had a convent upbringing. This emphasis was made in an attempt to vindicate the lady's reluctance and it showed, for the umpteenth time, just how little those who administer justice know about the facts of life beyond and outside the courts. When I was a lad everyone knew the form about convent girls and in, say, a dance hall, you always made a beeline for a girl wearing a crucifix. Any girl decorated with such a charm was considered to be a 'racing certainty' in the bedding stakes. A crucifix may well work at repelling vampires but I've never known one to keep a wolf at bay.

You don't have to be a professional writer or literary cocktail party habituée to know that Catholic lady writers dispense their favours in the most warm-hearted fashion, but I'm not, of course, knocking Catholics or women when I say this. In fact, I thank their God for them. If Ireland went on the pill then I think the place would be packed with sex exiles not tax exiles. The thing is, women have so little to interest them. What really revolts me is the way men behave in so far as it just isn't possible to be a womaniser without being a shit. It's in the very nature of the beast. A man who's easy to get to bed is a silly, foolish fellow. A man who has to pay for it is also a little daft although I can't help envying the fact that he can afford to, and that brings me to the amazing business — and I mean business — of the brothel at 32 Ambleside Avenue, Streatham. You'll recall that the police kept the place under surveillance for 12 days and saw 30 men a day going in at £15 a shot which the girls split 50-50 with Madame Payne, and those transactions came to £5,400 by my reckoning. Doubtless you'll agree with me when I say I now *know* I'm in the wrong business having suspected if for years. What I did love about the case was Mr Donald Farquarson QC saying that some of the women the police found in the house when they raided it were 'amateurs' and that they were 'raising money for household purchases or for Christmas'. Bless them. And who should want to stop them?

Again we have the bit about the law not being in touch with life — Madame got 18 months — although her clients included barristers and solicitors. The genius defending Madame said, in mitigation I assume, that the house in Ambleside Avenue was 'not an opulent New Orleans brothel', something I should have thought that anyone who knew how to spot the difference between Streatham and Louisiana could have told the judge.

Anyway, the laws concerning brothels were, as it was pointed out in court, made to protect women presumably because they can't protect themselves. Well, you could have fooled me or anyone else who has seen the creatures sitting in places like Annabel's festooned in diamonds. If the law wasn't an ass then surely it would legislate to protect men from the rapacious little beasts with, of course, double indemnity clauses where crucifix-wearing girls were concerned. There must be exceptions, I know, as I'm sure that hysterical girl Joan of Arc was one. Perhaps if she had been a little more outgoing she might have saved her skin. If she'd been tried this week in the Old Bailey she'd have been acquitted on the grounds of her convent upbringing.

DIRTY

There seems to be a touch of spring in the air. Yesterday, the 1981 Barclaycard arrived in the post and in the afternoon I escorted a lady to a sex shop. The Barclaycard gives me the most ridiculous and unrealistic feelings of security, and, as to the sex shop, I found it encouraging and comforting to know that it isn't only young and middle-aged men whose fancy lightly turns to thoughts of the next victim at around this time of year. Sadly, this particularly lady, an old flame barely flickering, intends to fly solo. I bumped into her, for the first time in an age, in the York Minster and she told me the story that we Soho lay-analysts are only too used to hearing. It seems she got married about three years ago and that her old man's passion has cooled somewhat since then. Would I, she asked me, accompany her to a sex shop where she intended to buy a vibrator, because she was too embarrassed to go in alone?

As we entered the shop in Old Compton Street, she gave a nervous giggle which was reciprocated by the Chinaman behind the counter and then we began to inspect the incredible implements. A sudden melancholy descended on me caused, I think, by an acute feeling of redundancy. I wandered off into another corner of the shop to browse through a vast tray of women's knickers and the cobwebbed vaults of my memory bank while the lady made her choice. It turned out to be a fairly modest choice made, I should guess, with the thought in the back of her mind that she should learn to walk before trying to run. That was somehow sad too. She clutched her wrapped up implement to her bosom, gave another embarrassed giggle, and I took her up to the Colony Room for a medicinal drink. It's quite extraordinary how women seem to go down the drain when they leave me, although I'm fully aware of the fact that it's unlikely any of them will ever see a vibrator stagger drunkenly through the front door at midnight. But last weekend I had a happier experience with an old flame burning, I fear, still a little too strongly for comfort. (These things should be finished cleanly, but I'm besotted.) Anyway, we went to Brighton for a couple of days — your old-fashioned English hotel ritual — and it's amazing how well you can get on with someone once you've stopped speaking to each other. But unlike the lady, Brighton has lost most of its charms, and why oh why did they kill off the Brighton Belle?

I liked Brighton better when it was a suburb of the East End populated largely by members of the underworld, racing spivs and assorted refugees from the law. It's odd to think that at one time criminals on the run went to Brighton to hide and not to Brazil. Now, it's rip-off antique shops and more homosexuals than I've seen at one gathering since I was 17 years old. One of them, a rather gross man called Rex who played Soho some 20 years ago, I saw helping a blind man across the road. The sea air must make for tranquillity because the Rex I knew spent more time duffing people up than he did helping them across anything bigger than a brandy. And the tranquillity was infectious. The lady and I gazed warmly at each other over the American Disaster hamburgers, held hands over the plaice and chips and offered each other no recriminations across the sweet and sour.

Only two things marred the idyll. A booklet called *What's*

On and Where In and Around Brighton which recommends every restaurant willy nilly and has the critical faculty of a compulsive first nighter and the fact that somewhere in Ireland — they hadn't caught him at that time — there lurked a mad Paddy of a Delilah who'd cut off the mane and tail of Storm Bird. Of course, there was one more thing. Presented with the hotel bill I suddenly realised why they're called 'dirty' weekends. One can only hope the cost of playing will keep the tourists away in their droves next summer.

In two or three weeks' time we're going to try a weekend in France. It's got to be cheaper. But wherever it is, I hope it's in the company of the old flame. It's harder to burn your fingers that way. Meanwhile, I shall turn once again to Valium because the nightmares concerning vibrators and Storm Birds are becoming unbearable.

CHILD BRIDE

'Yet teenage marriages can last' (*Radio Times*, 21 August 1979.)

Horace let himself in with his latchkey, walked into the hall and hung his satchel on the hatstand. The house seemed strangely quiet. He looked up the staircase and shouted. 'Mary, Mary, I'm home.' Nothing. Not a sound. He walked through to the kitchen and looked around. It was neat enough, spick and span indeed, but still no Mary. Then he saw it on the kitchen table propped up against a ketchup bottle. Her note. 'Your Mars Bar is in the oven. Love Mary XXX.'

Where the hell had she gone, he wondered. Probably over to Mavis's house he thought angrily. He sighed, sat down and pulled his battered paperback copy of *The Wind in the Willows* out of his blazer pocket and began to read. He couldn't concentrate. He put the book down and stared sulkily at the poster of John Travolta on the wall. 'Damn and bother,' he said aloud. They had only been married for three months and yet Mary still insisted that Thursday night was her night for going to Mavis's to play doctors and nurses. Well, tonight he'd have it out with her once and for all.

Later, he lay in bed sucking anxiously on a Cadbury sugar cigarette and staring at the exercise book that lay on his knee. 'Seges est ubi Troya erat.' Something was where Troy was all right, but what the hell was seges? Then he heard Mary opening the front door and then her voice. 'Cooee, it's me,' she called. 'About time too,' he muttered, under his breath. 'I'll be up in a minute darling,' she continued. 'I'm just going to wash out my gym slip.' God Almighty. Girls. What a soppy

lot they were, always washing something. Soon she was standing by the bed and looking down at him. 'I had an absolutely
super evening darling.' 'Oh yeah.' 'Well, aren't you interested?' He threw the exercise book off the bed and it landed on
his train set in the corner of the room. 'Of course I'm
interested.' 'Well Mavis pretended she had to have an
abortion and . . .' but Horace wasn't listening. He was
watching Mary who was slowly taking off her ankle socks. Just
below her right knee there was an old scar that was the result
of a hockey accident. It still excited him strangely and he
remembered the first time she had let him run his ink-stained
fingers over it.

Eventually, she stood there, undressed. Horace stared at
her, his eyes peeping over the eiderdown while he surrep-
titiously picked his nose beneath it. After she had finished
brushing her hair she began to put on her pyjamas with the
abrupt movements that excited him so. Twice she tripped over
and by now he wanted her so badly he had forgotten his acne.
She was wearing his favourite pyjamas — the ones with foxes
and geese on them — and then the wynceyette was beneath
his damp hands. Suddenly her body went rigid. 'Horace, for
God's sake,' she whispered, 'you know I've got maths in the
morning.' 'You've always got maths in the morning,' he said
trying to unbutton her pyjama jacket. 'Well, I have, I can't
help it, but I have. As a matter of fact we've got simultaneous
equations with Miss Harper.'

He turned away from her — angry, hurt and now cold.
He thought he loathed her and he wished to God he'd waited
until he was 15 before he'd got married. Eventually, the
silence between them was broken. 'Darling,' Mary whispered.
'What is it now?' he asked angrily. 'Well, I was thinking.
You know when Mallard broke the world speed record for a
steam driven engine?' 'What about it?' 'Was it in service with
the LMS or the LNER?' 'LNER, of course.' He reached out
for her. How could he hate her? They shared the same
interests. Railway engine numbers, hide and seek and shop-
lifting in Woolworths. It was his fault that they didn't get on
sometimes he thought. He shouldn't hurry their lovemaking
so much. She was, he thought, rather like a gobstopper. She

needed time. 'Will you still love me when I'm old?' she asked. 'Course I will,' he said. 'Even when we've taken our "O" levels?' 'Yes. Go to sleep.' He turned over. Tomorrow he would take her to Euston after school to see the 5.30 from Liverpool arrive at platform 3.

TOP DRAWERS

Although the Prix de L'Arc de Triomphe was a personal punting success for me I'm still very sorry that Troy didn't win the race for England. My sense of patriotism is, I'm afraid, based deeply in the realms of sport and, as we all know, sport is pretty trivial stuff. Nevertheless, I hate to see England beaten at cricket, I don't much like Irish horses sweeping the board at the Cheltenham Festival meeting and the spirit which gave us a 6-0 victory over the French at Trafalgar is continually bubbling up within me, like the ghastly, phoney self-pride exuded by a con-man. When I think of what Englishmen and women have done in the line of duty I just swell with pride.

In Manchester last week I saw something that made me so proud to be a member of this race it actually brought tears to my eyes. There's a pub there called Tommy Ducks — quite a nice pub — with some lovely old Victorian photographs on the wall and one of the most nourishing looking barmaids I've ever seen, but it's the ceiling of the place that staggered me. Pinned to it and covering the entire surface are approximately 500 pairs of women's knickers that were at one time removed from their owners on the premises.

Now although, of course, all civilised and sensible people and feminists must realise that this is common, vulgar, cheap and quite disgusting it is also rather remarkable. I wouldn't say that my eyes were exactly glued to the ceiling when I was in there but I was a little like a rabbit transfixed by car headlights. I suddenly felt that women were, after all, very wonderful people indeed. That 500 of them should have laid down their knickers in the cause of raising a North country smirk or two is wonderful proof of irrelevancies like the fact that there are, quite obviously, 500 women somewhere who don't read the *Guardian* women's page, 500 women somewhere that don't think men are *all* bad and 500 women it will, unfortunately, never be my pleasure to meet. They have slipped the net but they will be remembered.

I sat down at a table with a fairly revolting glass of wine, seating myself directly beneath the largest pair of cami-knickers I have ever seen that weren't directly enclosing a woman, and the tears just started to stream down my face. Admittedly I do have some pretty pressing problems at the moment but the tears I shed were shed, like those 500 knickers, from a sentimental but immediate joy. Think of those women. In their Rabelaisian lunch hours slurping over their gins and tonic, their ports and lemon, they upped their skirts and surrendered their last bastion of defence. To me, the picture didn't conjure up a sort of Coronation Street vulgarity, it evoked a Renoir-like vision of beauty and bliss. Where are they now, I wondered? What on earth has become of them? I had another glass of wine and that too turned to tears. I really felt for those ladies and I hoped that they had continued on life's rough road without ever having made the mistake of removing other pairs of knickers for the wrong men.

You must see, as I did, in that sudden flash of plonk-induced reality, that the 600 who rode into the valley of death were nothing compared to the 500 who laid down their drawers in Tommy Ducks. Balaclava palled beside Manchester. At closing time, last orders seemed so poignant beneath that heaven of knickers that I stood, along with three miners, an engineer and six Manchester United supporters, in silence and at attention and we remembered them. From the early dawn chorus of scraping toast to the midnight call of 'Where the hell have you been all bloody day?' we remembered them.